THOUGHTS
ON THE FUNDING SYSTEM

Also published in

REPRINTS OF ECONOMIC CLASSICS

By 'Piercy Ravenstone'

A FEW DOUBTS AS TO THE CORRECTNESS OF
SOME OPINIONS GENERALLY ENTERTAINED
ON THE SUBJECTS OF POLITICAL ECONOMY
AND POPULATION [1821]

THOUGHTS

ON THE

FUNDING SYSTEM

AND ITS EFFECTS

BY

PIERCY RAVENSTONE

[1824]

REPRINTS OF ECONOMIC CLASSICS

AUGUSTUS M. KELLEY · PUBLISHERS
NEW YORK · 1966

Library of Congress Catalogue Card Number
66 - 28961

PRINTED IN THE UNITED STATES OF AMERICA
by SENTRY PRESS, NEW YORK, N. Y. 10019

THOUGHTS

ON THE FUNDING SYSTEM.

THOUGHTS

ON THE

FUNDING SYSTEM,

AND

ITS EFFECTS.

I had rather be a kitten, and cry mew,
Than one of these same *System-mongers*.
HENRY IV.

By PIERCY RAVENSTONE, M.A.

LONDON:
PRINTED FOR
J. ANDREWS, 167, NEW BOND-STREET,
AND J. M. RICHARDSON, CORNHILL.

MDCCCXXIV.

THOUGHTS ON THE FUNDING SYSTEM,

&c. &c.

THE events of the last hundred years, the changes they have wrought in the mode of existence of every nation of Europe, and the complexity they have introduced into all the relations of society, have given to the science of political economy an importance to which it could never before pretend. As the classes into which nations are divided have been multiplied, as the space allotted to the motions of each individual have been more circumscribed, their different interests have brought men more frequently into collision, and it has required no small share of skill to state and regulate the pretensions of each. It is not, therefore, to be wondered at, however much it may be matter of regret, that in discussions so intricate and often so perplexed, the true principles should be lost sight of on which society is formed, and which alone, by the general happiness they produce, can make amends for its laws and restrictions, and the abridgment of natural freedom that it necessarily brings in its train.

Among all the relations of society, what may be called its financial relations are almost the last to attract attention. It is only in a high state of civilization, when the idle classes have become numerous and powerful, that men occupy themselves with the best means of increasing and distributing a nation's wealth. Private interest is the great stimulus to improvement. The public good is seldom

much thought of till it can be turned into the stream of
individual advantage. It is never pursued with so much
eagerness as when it can be made a pretext for jobs, when
corruption can be sanctioned by its name.

In a country where land is the only property, and its rents
and the profits which arise from their expenditure the only
source of revenue, as there can be no mystery, as there is
no room for contrivance, men are not very solicitous to inquire into the causes of the wealth of nations, nor into
the best manner of disposing of their savings. As they see
that all the productions of the earth are of a perishable
nature, and have no value but what they derive from consumption, as they perceive that the only use of manufactures is to increase comforts, and to offer a more compen-
dious and more refined mean of expenditure; they do not
comprehend how it is possible for accumulation to take
place. Where there is no fund in which savings can be laid
up, to save seems in reality to waste. What is not consumed can only be thrown away. True wisdom, they think,
and they think rightly, can only consist in well-regulated
enjoyment: their industry can never be well employed but
when it adds to their comforts.

Such is necessarily the state of every people who have
created no public debt: such was the condition of all the
nations of Europe before their governments had thought of
the ingenious expedient of mortgaging the public revenues.
They lived carelessly from day to day, enjoying the good
whilst they had it, and opposing nothing to extraordinary
difficulties when they came but extraordinary privations.
The calls of the public, the necessities of a war, only put
down for a time the extravagance of private luxury. The
servants and retainers of the gentry were converted into
soldiers, and the nobleman when he harnessed on his armour
broke up every thing that was expensive in his establishment. A war caused no new expense, it only gave another

direction to what already took place. The gentry were a militia always bound to obey the call of the nation: their estates were their stipend, which they spent as they pleased when not required for the service of the country, to whom they paid their rent by assuring to it security.

The funding system, by creating a new and undefinable species of property, which neither held of the land nor yet of the industry of the country, which had no local existence, no tangible being, not only overthrew the whole scheme of society, but gave a new turn to men's ideas. No bounds could be assigned to a nation's wealth when new fortunes might be created without taking away from those that already existed. The power of accumulation bestowed on individuals appeared to be conferred on the whole community. Where wealth grew with so much rapidity, there seemed no difficulty in anticipating its growth, and supplying the wants of to-day by the means of to-morrow. The scheme could not but be agreeable to all the stirring spirits to whom it opened the road to fortune. Others without any views of interest were led away by the charm of words. The borrowing from posterity, as it was called, was so happy an expression, it was so full of vagueness and uncertainty, that it could not but generate confusion, and give birth to a thousand absurdities in reasoning. When men had once persuaded themselves that they could spend immediately what was only to exist hereafter, they could have no difficulty in believing that they might save what had already ceased to exist. One false consequence led to another. Though they were usually adventurers who grew rich by these revolutions of fortune, yet as men saw capital every where fastening on industry to share in the produce of its labour, they concluded that it was capital gave all its activity to industry. Though they saw fortunes raised during wars, which were again dissipated in time of peace, they chose, in deference to the common sense of

mankind, but in defiance of their own principles, to consider war as a destroyer of capital, which could only be accumulated by the arts of peace.

These reasonings proceeding from false premises, as they
could not fail to involve in a labyrinth of perplexities all
those who had no other guide than common sense, soon
raised political economy to the rank of a science. From
that moment, as might be expected, every day added to the
darkness with which it was surrounded, every new treatise
only sunk it deeper in obscurity. They who though un-
initiated in its mysteries have been accustomed to watch
the progress of science, cannot but be aware how readily
learned men in their inquiries content themselves with
words, and what a natural abhorrence they have of whatever bears the stamp of common sense. As their chief object is to distinguish themselves from the great herd of men
who are busied with things, they delight in abstractions,
they choose words for their province. Certain cabalistical
terms are introduced into the sciences, which are to silence
all inquiries. It is not expected that the adept should
understand them, it is enough that he can repeat them.
No useful invention owes its birth to science; it seems
the business of learned men to disguise under hard
names, and to render obscure the simple discoveries of
genius.

Political economy, as it was peculiarly obnoxious to its
baleful influence, was not likely to escape unhurt from this
tendency to jargon, which science has heaped up to encumber all the avenues to knowledge. There is something in
the nature of the abstract sciences that stops pretenders on
the threshold. The very terms of the mathematics are re-
pulsive; signs tangents and co-efficients are quite appalling
to those who have never used their minds to steady application. The catechism of chemistry is not more enticing; as
it cannot be acquired without a considerable effort of me-

mory, it sets at defiance all desultory studies. Poetry is
secured by other safeguards. Its popular character, which
has rescued it from mystery, and the ridicule which follows
on any unsuccessful attempt, deters the sober and the timid,
and leave it to the unheeded pursuit of the rash and the
successful cultivation of those who really feel the impulse
of genius. Political economy has none of these securities
against the inroads of ignorance and pretension. It seems to
treat of the every-day occurrences of life; its terms are in
common use ; its language is that which is familiar in the
world. The man who has spent all his days in getting and
spending money easily fancies himself competent to decide
on the nature of wealth and its consumption. He seems to
be only generalizing his own experience, and embodying
his own reflections. In an age of literary pretension,
where every man is obliged, at least in appearance, to know
something, political economy has accordingly become the
study of all those who felt themselves unequal to other pursuits. It was the peaceful province of acrostic land where
they whose courage cowered before higher enterprise might
yet hope to acquire a comfortable renown. No fiery dragons
were placed to guard its treasures—no fearful monsters
rendered dangerous their approach ; there was nothing in
the adventure to dishearten the most recreant knight.

The wonderful has irresistible charms for ignorance.
Narrow minds cannot conceive the simplicity of true knowledge; nothing seems to them worth knowing that is not
strange and mysterious. They have no taste for the simple
processes of nature, they cannot relish them till they are
seasoned and disguised by the hard words of science. Like
the Bourgeois gentilhomme, they cannot persuade themselves that men's every-day talk is prose; that art is but
the handmaid of Nature to follow and imitate her works,
not to suggest them. The less they comprehend of doctrines, the more they are in opposition to generally-received

notions, the more in their eyes they bear the stamp of genius. Learned words with them sanctify the greatest absurdities ; they readily yield their assent to propositions, when veiled under the garb of science, which in their natural state would stagger their belief.

Hence into political economy, which is essentially a science of calculation which treats of visible and tangible objects, which is principally conversant with facts, have been introduced, all the refinements and all the subtleties of metaphysics. The broad processes of nature have been lost sight of under the cobwebs of sophistry. Discussions have been pursued with all the eagerness of the most angry polemics, hardly less absurd than those which once made it a question, whether the mendicant friars had a property or only a usufruct in the food they ate. He was the greatest authority, his fame was most widely spread, who dealt most largely in distinctions without a difference. The narrow views which such limited intellects would necessarily take of their subject, has not tended a little to create confusion. They generalized too fast. As children in their first attempts to classify their ideas, call every man they meet papa, so they erected the results of their individual experience into general laws. Because a thing was, they thought it could not be otherwise. The anomalies which in every country are created by the artificial regulations of men, they confounded with the great principles which govern and uphold the world. The abuses of society were to them as sacred as its primary and fundamental institutions. As they judged of the wisdom of nature by what to them seemed wisdom in the municipal regulations by which they were surrounded, they made her responsible for the follies and crimes of men. Political economy thus treated became perverted in all her principles. She was made the close ally of self-interest and corruption ; it was in the armory of her terms that tyranny and oppression found their deadliest weapons. She has oftener been called in as an auxiliary, when abuses were to be accounted for and justified than when their origin was to be detected and their remedy suggested. The most oppressive governments have been those which have most earnestly cultivated this science, for it has tended to give stability to misrule, by lending it the support of system, and shrouding its deformities under the semblance of wisdom. The doctrine of capital and its effects is indeed the most injurious to society that ever was broached. To teach that the wealth and power of a nation depend on its capital, is to make industry ancillary to riches, to make men subservient to property. Where such a system is allowed to prevail, the greater part of the people must be, under whatever name disguised, merely *adscripti glebæ*. Their situation will be without comfort and without hope ; they will be doomed to toil, not for their own benefit, but for that of their masters. All rights will belong to the rich, all duties will be left to the poor. The people will be made to bow their necks beneath the yoke of the harshest of all rules, the aristocracy of wealth.

From the errors into which men have fallen by not distinguishing the rights of industry from those of property, by looking on men but as the means of cultivation, has arisen the much debated question, which is most advantageous to a nation, to borrow, during the war, the means of carrying it on, or to employ the intervals of peace in laying up what is needful for the prosecution of future hostilities ; whether a people shall begin by spending, that it may afterwards accumulate, or begin by heaping up the means of future expense. Treated solely as a question of finance, as it has hitherto been, the problem is deserving of little attention, it is but a question of words. All its importance arises from the influence which the different practices may have on the happiness and freedom of a people In these discussions it has been assumed, without the least shadow of proof, that it is possible for a whole nation to accumulate, not in the true sense of adding every day to the comforts of every class of the people, but in the more popular sense of laying by a part of its income, of producing more than it consumes. It is not surprising that a position which seems warranted by every man's experience should have been so generally admitted. Men are for ever deluded by similitudes : there is no more frequent source of error than a mistaken analogy. What each individual of a community is certainly capable of doing, it seemed equally easy for the community in its corporate capacity to do. In the hurry and bustle of active life, where each man's attention is absorbed in his own pursuits, the great and rooted distinction between the two cases is so wrapped up in extraneous circumstances as to be wholly lost sight of : in the ordinary intercourse of individuals the property that one man acquires another as surely loses. One man cannot buy an estate but because another sells it. Acquisition is in reality only transfer. To a whole people it is therefore impossible. They may add to their produce, they may increase their consumption, they may swell the amount of their comforts, they may wanton in new luxuries, but they cannot lay by. This mistake, however, singular as it is, is much less extraordinary than that of the opponents of accumulation, the advocates of the funding system. In pretending to stave off the expenses of the present hour to a future day, in contending that you can burthen posterity to supply the wants of the existing generation, they in reality assert the monstrous proposition that you can consume what does not yet exist, that you can feed on provisions before their seeds have been sown in the earth. If these doctrines had been confined to the schools, their mistakes, as they would have been harmless, might have been amusing. But in the mouths of statesmen, they become of quite another importance. Mixed up with all its laws and

institutions, new modelling the opinions of judges and
warping the very principles of justice, (which, immutable
as they are said to be, will still, so long as they are administered by men, be swayed by the caprice of fashion)
they exercise a dreadful influence on the happiness of a
nation. Its constitution perishes, whilst all its forms remain entire. The greatest innovators are found amongst
the steadiest enemies of reform.

As this doctrine of capital and the wonderful effects of
accumulation are the basis of all modern political economy,
as it is the key-stone which holds together all the discordant
parts of the funding system, it will not be a waste of time
to examine it in detail. If it can be shewn that it is not
possible for a nation either to save or to anticipate its
revenues ; if it can be shewn that all that is produced must
be consumed at the very time of production, and that nothing can be consumed till it has been first produced ; the
whole merits and demerits of the funding system will stand
confessed before us. Posterity will appear to be wholly
uninterested in the acts of the present generation : all their
good and all their evil will be for those who have committed
them. Borrowing will not have diminished the expense of
the present day, nor have added to that of time to come.
All the wisdom of our statesmen will have ended in a great
transfer of property from one class of persons to another,
in creating an enormous fund for the reward of jobs and
peculation.

In considering how small a proportion of every civilized
society, even when regulated with most wisdom, is employed in productive industry, and that every step in civilization lessens even that small proportion ; in observing
how many of our fellow creatures seem only born to consume the fruits of the earth ; what waste and extravagance
attends the expenditure of the rich ; slight thinkers are in-
sensibly led to conclude that if in any country all laboured and

all lived with frugality, the accumulation of wealth must be prodigious ; and as they have seen that in all individual instances power follows wealth, they infer that the power of such a nation would keep pace with its riches. But wealth and power are wholly relative terms, they have no positive existence ; all their value is derived from the poverty and weakness of others. It is useless for one man to have too much, his superfluity would add nothing to his influence unless there were others who had too little. It is their wants which constitute his wealth. In England, as every man employed in productive labour produces five times as much as he consumes, his means greatly exceed his wants. If then every man laboured, all would be seemingly rich, for each would have five times as much as he had need of. But this apparent wealth would ill disguise his real poverty. When all were equal, none would labour for another. The necessaries of life would be over abundant whilst its comforts were entirely wanting. The greater part of each man's labour would be in vain, for there would be none to consume its produce. His toil would bring him no relaxation ; he would have nothing but what he owed to the labour of his own hands. Men's actions, however, are generally wiser than their words ; they seldom act up to their theories ; feeling corrects the errors of their reasoning. Though moralists have disserted, time out of mind, on the advantages of industry ; though thousands of volumes have been written to prove that employment is necessary to happiness, a natural instinct teaches them that the worth of industry consists entirely in its consequences, and that where labour brings no reward, it is better to be idle than to be uselessly employed, to do no nothing than to labour in vain.

On this principle, society has been constructed, its progress has every where followed this law. In the early stages of association, when men, bound together by few ties, contribute little to each other's aid, it is as much as each can do with all his industry to keep himself from starving. The life of the savage, who subsists by hunting, has sometimes been described as a life of idleness, and it may seem so to those who have only seen him when unemployed. But his repose is not that of indolence, it is called for by exhaustion : it is the consequence of severe fatigues and privations. His intervals of sloth are rendered necessary by the intensity of his labours. He throws himself on the ground to recover new strength for the chase. In every subsequent stage of society, as increased numbers and better contrivances add to each man's power of production, the number of those who labour is gradually diminished. What is more than is required for the maintenance of those who toil, is reserved for the support of a portion of the society which is allowed to live in idleness. Property grows from the improvement of the means of production ; its sole business is the encouragement of idleness. When each man's labour is barely sufficient for his own subsistence, as there can be no property, there will be no idle men. When one man's labour can maintain five, there will be four idle men for one employed in production : in no other way can the produce be consumed.

As the object of society is to magnify the idle at the expense of the industrious, to create power out of plenty, this state of things is not always apparent. Social institutions are ever labouring to confound the industry which is employed in consumption with that primary industry whose duty it is to produce, the industry which waits on property with that from which it derives its existence. Indeed the first, as it gives to a state its splendour and magnificence, as from it rulers derive all their greatness, is usually considered as the most valuable. To increase a nation's modes of expenditure is supposed to add to its wealth. Yet no two things can be more distinct in their

nature than these two species of industry. The industry
which produces is the parent of property ; that which aids
consumption is its child. This is always busy in pulling
down what that is as constantly building up. It is, however, the industry of consumption, which, by a strange perversion of reasoning, political economy has chosen to consider as the source of the wealth of nations. Trade and
manufactures, which grow with a nation's growth, whose
increase necessarily keeps pace with every improvement in
the employment of its industry, which are in reality only a
channel to make expense more easy, have been looked on
as the cause of that prosperity they only follow. To artificial regulations, to the contrivances of men, have been
attributed that power of expansion, that elasticity of nature,
which is interwoven in the very texture of society. Men
cannot turn their industry to produce the comforts and
luxuries of life but because it is not wanted to produce what
is necessary to existence. The refinements of life only
begin to be thought of when no more labour can be usefully
employed in its necessities. Every improvement in the
power of production is the parent of a new manufacture.
Where each man's labour is barely sufficient to procure his
own subsistence, none can be employed in luxuries. As
there could be none who would supply them with food,
none to whom they could sell their useless industry, the pro-
fessors of such arts must starve. This is, therefore, from
the very nature of things, the regular progress of society.
As soon as increased numbers have allowed of these improvements in the employment of industry which make a
man's labour sufficient for the maintenance of more than
his own family, the hopeless scheme of accumulation is not
thought of, but the surplus is assigned to the maintenance
of some portion of the society who are permitted to live in
idleness. Property is thus created, which is continually
increasing with every improvement in the skill and industry

with which labour is conducted. In a state of society where one man's labour can only support two families, the gross produce of the country will be shared equally between its industry and its property ; where increased skill enables one man to maintain five, four parts will constitute the property of the country, one only will be reserved for the maintenance of its industry. In the one case the idle men and their dependents will form one half of the nation; in the other, four fifths of the people will be comprised in these classes. It is this growth of property, this greater ability to maintain idle men, and unproductive industry, that in political economy is called capital. But this increase of capital may be without any addition to a nation's wealth. Where the growth of society is allowed to follow its natural course, every improvement of the powers of industry will add to the comforts of the whole community ; as more will be produced, each man may consume more. But when artificial regulations force the growth of property too fast, improved industry, instead of adding to the amount of production, only lessens the number of producers. The capital of such a country will be always increasing, whilst the real wealth of a nation, the comforts and happiness of the people, will be as rapidly diminishing. The unnatural growth of the idle will stunt and dwarf the industrious ; when too much nourishment is bestowed on the belly, the limbs lose their strength. But property which is wholly impotent in encouraging productive industry, and is sometimes hurtful to it, is all powerful in creating the industry of consumption. As the idle are the great consumers of the luxuries of life, trade and manufactures will be in proportion not to a nation's wealth, but to the amount of its property. They will grow fastest where the condition of the people is worst. As the destination of property is expense, as without that it is wholly useless to its owner, its existence is intimately connected with that of the industry of consumption. Like those mysterious beings we read of in eastern tales, one soul animates the two bodies; the one cannot die but the other perishes. They both, however, owe their life to the same parent. They are the offspring of productive industry, they are its nurse-children, and are fed from its breast; their health depends on its vigour; it cannot languish but it spreads their bed of sickness, it cannot pass away but it tolls their parting knell.

Property is in reality but a rent charge on productive industry. It cannot increase the quantity of industry, for the very condition of its existence is a superabundance of produce. As consumption is the purpose for which it is created, to that alone it can be devoted. As it increases with every increase of population and every improvement in the management of labour, it is continually outgrowing the natural wants of those to whom providence has assigned the right of living in idleness on the labours of their fellow creatures. The lord of boundless empires cannot in his own person consume more than the poorest of his subjects. The same quantity of food will satisfy his hunger; he does not require more clothing to protect him from the inclemency of the weather. He is compelled, therefore, to imagine artificial wants, to hire others to help in consuming his superfluities. This is the origin of all manufactures; they owe their existence to the necessity which the rich feel of consuming by the means of others that part of the produce of the earth which is too much for their own consumption; none of them contribute to the existence of man, they are only conversant with his artificial wants. They cannot add to the wealth of a people, they only furnish easier means of expenditure. Their amount is dependant on the success of productive industry. They are the superfluities of the cultivator which reward the manufacturer and enable him to live. If each man's labour were but enough to procure his own food, there could be no property, and no part of a people's industry could be turned away to work for the wants of the imagination. In every case, however, accumulation is equally impossible. As consumption is the only purpose of production, it necessarily regulates its amount, for it gives it all its value. The labour that is employed on useless things is entirely thrown away. They who are so occupied might as well be idle; they have in reality only been busy about nothing. Houses that there were none to inhabit would only encumber the earth: corn that there were none to eat, clothes that there were none to wear, would soon become the prey of the weevil and the moth. Instead of adding to men's wealth, they would only increase their plagues. To hoard is the wisdom of a jackdaw; to multiply his enjoyments, that of a reasonable creature.

But whilst the uselessness of saving what perishes in the moment of accumulation be admitted, there will be those who, whilst they allow the inability of trade and manufactures to increase a nation's property, will contend that there are other objects of a less perishable nature, whose use is of all times and all countries; that hoards of the precious metals may be made to any amount without losing any of their value. This scheme is, however, as bottomless as the other. The government of a state may indeed place itself in the situation of the idle men; by drawing to itself all the revenues of the country it may annihilate their existence; it may determine that all who are not occupied with the industry of production shall be employed in working for gold or silver, either directly, or if the country has no mines, in producing objects that may be exchanged with those nations that have. It is clear that a country directing all its industry to such a purpose might amass a treasure of almost any conceivable magnitude. Its amount might render trifling even Dr. Price's most visionary conceptions. Nor would the industry of the country receive any check whilst this abstraction of capital was going forward. Every man would be employed either in producing the necessaries of life or the means of purchasing gold and silver. The demand of the state would supply the want of individual consumption; the riches of the nation would make up for the poverty of private persons. As there would be no idle men, as the industry of all would be in constant activity, the amount of production would greatly exceed that of other nations where a large portion of the people are only employed in consumption, and its wealth, as it would not be consumed, would become almost boundless. But such is the fallacy of all human reasoning, that this accumulation, which on the principles of political economy should make a nation great and powerful, would only deprive the people of all comforts without adding to the power of the state. All this excess of industry would be only labour lost. Gold and silver, even more than other objects, as they administer only to the artificial wants of men, have but a conventional value. As they cannot themselves be applied to any useful purpose, their worth depends entirely on the means which people have of indulging in fancies. So long as they are only produced in proportion to the artificial wants of society, their value is estimated by the labour it has cost to procure them. The gold which it has taken ten days' labour to raise will exchange against the cloth which it has occupied the weaver ten days to make. Increase, however, the precious metals beyond what the state of society demands, and they become of no more value than stones. None will give the necessaries of life for a superabundance of superfluities. A country thus overloaded with treasure would be in the situation of a besieged town, where the inhabitants may be dying of hunger whilst every bank is overflowing with gold and silver. An enormous hoard in the hour of danger would be found wholly inoperative to defend a country. As soon as it came to be used, it would destroy its own value. As all the surplus industry of the country will have been employed in its acquisition, there will be nothing against which it can exchange. Rub off the high polish which the imagination of avarice gives to the precious metals, and they shew but dross. To hoard them up serves but, like all other accumulation, to display their worthlessness.

Its numbers, not its riches, constitute a nation's strength. Men and the means of feeding them are all that war requires. It is only as an agent in procuring them that money is of any value. If the men and their subsistence do not already exist, no money can create them. If they do exist, a nation, whatever may be the amount of its treasure, can only do what the poorest of its neighbours can and would equally do, it will divert a part of its population from the industry of consumption to the purposes of war. In so doing, however, the people amongst whom industry is conducted with most skill, will have a decided advantage. As a smaller proportion of the population will be required for production, a greater number can be spared for defence. In modern society, indeed, this advantage is more than compensated by the inequality of fortunes and the increase of fictitious wealth. Its possessors, who exercise a controlling influence over the government, embarrass all its operations by their unwillingness to part with any of their means of luxury. Since the gentry no longer constitute the militia of the country, since their retainers have ceased to form its armies, they insist that soldiers shall be found without lessening the number of servants, that the means of paying them shall not diminish their expense. The nation, therefore, which has least artificial wealth is always that which can send forth the largest hosts. Where there are habitually no idlers, it is easiest to create them. Where the exactions of property are least, industry has most to spare from its daily earnings. It was the destruction of the nobility, of the clergy, of the finances of France, that covered her soil with soldiers. With no treasure, and no credit, she balanced the resources of all Europe ; for she could bring into the field all her idle men.

Hoarding has been so little the habit of states, that it is not easy to reason from the past. The few examples that occur certainly do not favour the practice. The princes of antiquity, who laid by treasures, do not seem to have added to their means of defence. Money with them never proved the sinews of war. The gold and silver of its kings only enabled their conquerors to carry the wealth of Asia with more ease to Rome. The Italian Republics of the middle ages indeed waged war solely with money ; their armies were entirely filled with mercenaries ; their citizens fought but with their purses. But the constitution of these states was so peculiar that their example cannot be drawn into a precedent. They were not nations ; they were only guilds of traders, with no property but what they derived from their traffic. Possessed of no territory, with them there was no productive industry; theirs was the industry of consumption, which, administering to artificial wants, lives but by the plunder of the world. As their incomes were not derived from the soil they could not be spent in its productions. The hiring of stranger soldiers was the only way in which they could employ the profits they made from foreigners. What they gained as traders they were forced to lose as sovereigns. They were but the channels through which the Swiss and the Germans and the Mountaineers of Italy applied their surplus produce to the maintenance of idlers. What Florence gained from them by trade she gave back to them for protection. It was not, however, from accumulation that she drew her means. She acquired no territory ; her profits were never realized in land ; her treasury was never filled with gold and silver ; her palaces, her pictures, her statues, were not easily convertible into the food of war. Her growing gains supplied her expenditure. What she got from foreigners with one hand she gave back with the other. It was from necessity her armies were filled with strangers ; it was only in their persons the poorer debtors could discharge the balance of their trading transactions. It was not that Florence had not citizens, and that her citizens were not able and willing to fight. But the consumption of a country in native produce can never exceed the amount of production. That part of a nation's revenue which is derived from foreigners must, in some way or other, be spent on foreigners. As every thing that is produced forms income to somebody, the income derived from national resources must always be equal in amount to all the national commodities. The income derived from foreign sources can only be met by foreign produce. Such an income is usually dissipated in foreign luxuries ; but the sumptuary laws which forbad this kind of expense compelled Florence to dabble in war. As she was not allowed to consume the goods of those with whom she dealt, she was forced to hire their persons.

This state of things was not peculiar to Florence. The trade and migrations of half the people of the world are regulated on the same principle. Ireland sends her surplus produce to pay the rents of her landlords in England, and her surplus poor follow to consume it. Switzerland hires out her children to the neighbouring nations, and she accumulates her savings in the imaginary wealth of foreign funds in debts which are never to be paid. When Holland was the broker of other nations, when much of her income was derived from the funds of other states, her soldiers and her servants, the ministers of her state, and her luxury, were nearly all foreigners. The stream of wealth which the tribute of Mexico and Peru poured into the bosom of Spain contributed nothing to feed her native industry. By withdrawing a larger portion of her people from productive industry, it served but to encourage luxury and its never failing companion—wretchedness. That part of her income which exceeded her own produce was necessarily spent abroad. Spain in the fulness of her riches was overrun with idlers and beggars. As she drew from foreigners a part of her riches, she unavoidably became dependant on them for a part of her subsistence. Had she never possessed the mines of Potosi she had never wanted the corn of Poland. Since she has lost her transatlantic provinces she has almost ceased to import grain. They who can no longer derive a subsistence from the tribute of America, are forced to gain their livelihood by the exertion of their own industry. With her artificial wealth have disappeared her artificial wants.

These examples may satisfy us that by no ordinary process can accumulation be brought about. It can only happen when the usual march of society is interrupted, and when the government, putting itself in the place of the gentry of a country, draws to itself a greater share of its revenues than are needed for the purposes of government. Violent as such a measure seems to be, its financial consequences would be wholly unimportant to the nation at large; it would neither take from nor add to the wealth of the nation; it would but give a different direction to its industry. The useless accumulation which now takes place in the hands of individuals in the shape of buckles and buttons, of pictures and statues, would then take place in the hands of the state in equally useless heaps of sovereigns or Napoleons, which, as soon as they exceeded the wants of society, would, like the buttons and buckles, there were none to wear, be wholly without value.

But the dread of this evil need not haunt our apprehensions. The government of every country is in the hands of the rich, and though power delights in riding a hobby-horse, they will hardly indulge in an amusement that will lessen their own importance, and perhaps destroy their existence. They will find no pleasure in hoards which can

only be made at their own expense. The fascinations of
the Funding System will be more difficult to resist. Their
anxiety to throw the burden from their own shoulders
will blind them to its consequences, and will lead them to
cherish the useless and extravagant expenditure of which it
is at the same time the cause and the consequence—an expenditure not less destructive of the existing property of
a country, though in its effects it may be perhaps not without advantage to society. But its workings are silent and
unperceived. As for every rich man it pulls down it raises
up a new one, as it does not destroy property, but only
transfer it, its operation is not distinctly felt. Amidst the
growing wealth of the prosperous, the poverty that assails
individuals is but little heeded.

It is not, however, alone to ignorance of its tendency
that the Funding System owes its general adoption. Other
causes have contributed their full share. It was the
easiest way of throwing the burthens of the country from its
property on its industry. Modern politicians indeed contend that taxes on articles of consumption are not taxes on
industry ; that to increase the cost of his bread, of his beer,
of his soap, of his candles, is no injury to the labourer ;
that the increased expense of his subsistence is only paid
nominally by himself, but really by his employer ; that as
the wages of labour are never more than are absolutely
necessary for the subsistence of the labourer, and as they
can never be less, if the expense of his living be increased,
the amount of his wages must be so likewise. If this atrocious doctrine, which reduces the greater part of the human race to the wretched condition of beasts of burden,
whose wants and comforts are to be cared for only so far
as is beneficial to their owner, had been generally true, no
taxes would ever have been imposed on articles of consumption. If property had felt that the charge fell ultimately on itself, it would never have allowed it to come
circuitously, augmented by all the expense of collection,

and swelled in amount by all the profits of all the different tradesmen through whose hands it passed; it would have preferred direct taxation as attended with least expense. But it is not true that the wages of labour are never more than is sufficient to support the labourer. In countries where wages are very low, the labour of the workman is very small. He receives as much in proportion to what he does, as when it is most dearly paid. Wages are always regulated by the value of the work done in the general market of the world. The buyer does not inquire the cost of the goods, but their worth. A bushel of German wheat is in every part of the world worth as much as a bushel of English wheat. But, if rent and taxes be less in Germany than in England, and the profits of the farmer be much more moderate, if a smaller part of the produce be directed to other purposes, more will remain to the labourer. If he does not gain it in higher wages, he will gain it in diminished labour and diminished expenses. Where the produce of the land sells for little, it costs but little to live. This equality of earnings is especially noticeable in the wages of artisans. They who have compared the manufactures of England with those of other countries, know that the foreign workman is as dearly paid as the English. If in the course of the year he receives less, it is because his employment, being less constant, he has done less work. Here, however, is a fund for taxation that does not fall on property. Increase the workman's expense of living, and, as he cannot add to the price of his article, he will increase the quantity of his labour. This he will be enabled to do without overloading the market with his peculiar industry; for, as whatever is raised by taxes goes to the maintenance of idle men, every additional tax, whilst it increases the number of consumers, lessens the number of workmen. The causes which compel him to do more work add in exactly the same proportion to the number of his customers. It is evident, however, that this power of increasing his labour is not without bounds. It never can exceed his physical strength. As it is easier to imagine new taxes than to invent new improvements for the abridgment of labour, it is seldom that the exertions of genius can keep pace with the contrivances of the Exchequer. In our own country this fund of reserved industry, which has stood our financiers in such good stead, seems wholly exhausted. In the last hundred years, since the invention of the Funding System, the expense of living to the artisan has more than doubled, whilst the price paid for his labour has undergone no alteration. Where labour is paid by the piece, the rates have not varied; where it is paid by the day, more work is required from the labourer. Our workmen are kept habitually in such a state of exertion, that no pressure can compel them to greater efforts. No saints' days allure them to idleness, no wakes, no holydays, are allowed to break in on their never-ceasing employment. The sun that rises on their toil goes down on their unfinished labours. The unbroken industry of six days afford but the bare means of existence. The artificial price which unjust laws have given to corn have reduced the wages of the labourer to the lowest sum on which he can subsist. The increase of poor-rates which immediately follows even the smallest rise in the cost of provisions, cannot leave a doubt that farther taxes on industry are impracticable; that it is impossible to extract more from the wretchedness of the people. The spell of the tax-gatherer has lost its charm. The time is gone by when the rich might be lavish of taxation; when under the hypocritical pretence of caring for the people's morals, they might vote a tax on beer or on spirits without any expense to themselves; when the burthen of taxation was for the poor, its advantages, all the jobs it caused and justified, were for their representatives. Whatever burthens are now imposed must fall on the property of the country. Nothing can be given to taxes but what is taken from rent. The public mind has accordingly taken a new turn. Men begin to calculate more accurately the effect of the Funding System. Private interest easily gains the attention which was denied to the public good. So long as borrowing only pressed on the poor, so long as its worst consequences were only the reducing to beggary the great body of the people, it was hailed as a measure fraught with public good. But the moment its effects become harmless, the moment the worst crimes it can achieve is the transfer of property from one set of useless men to another equally useless, all its defects and all its vices are immediately discovered. It becomes an object of abhorrence for what was before the subject of praise.

There was a time, when such was the infatuation in men's minds, it might have been necessary to prove that a national debt adds nothing to a nation's wealth. They who made the riches of a people consist in the amount of its unproductive industry, who considered trade and manufactures as sources of wealth, were likely enough to fall into this error; to confound the increase of rich men with the increase of riches. They who had been taught, that the increase of property, which is often but the abuse of society, was its only end, were justified in considering the Funding System as beneficial to a nation, since it added a new class of rich men, without taking away from the means of those who already existed. The misery it inflicted on the great body of the people they did not see, and they did not care for. Lost in abstraction, they could not descend to realities. The wealth of the nation was their object, not the comfort and happiness of the people; and provided the quantity of fustians, and callicoes, and muslins, and broad-cloths, was augmented, it mattered not to them by what privations of the people this result was obtained. As long as men shut their eyes to the perishable nature of every object which either nature or art produces—as long as they would not see that it is consumption which, by giving them all their value, regulates the amount even of manufactures, they were not likely to discover that the produce of every nation must in all cases be in proportion to the population it is to support; that to force a greater production would only be to throw away labour; that the manner in which a nation's income is distributed, determines indeed the quality, but in no way the quantity, of its produce.

But the delusion is fast wearing away. Light begins to break into the minds of men. The importunate demands of the tax-gatherer, and the clamour of breaking tenants, have waked them from their dreams of evergrowing riches, by dinning in their ears, in a tone that admits of no misconception, that what is taken for national purposes is so much subtracted from individual income; that the more idle men are retained by the nation, the fewer can be allowed for the splendour of private life. The Funding System is no longer lauded as beneficial to a nation, necessity is urged as an excuse for its creation. Our heavy debt is no longer a source of wealth, it is no longer appealed to as a proof of our riches, it has at last become an unavoidable evil. The land-owners admit, that the national resources are crippled, that a part of the cargo has been thrown overboard, but it was for the good of the remainder; had the vessel not been lightened, she must have gone down.

This position is not more tenable than the other. Inquiry will convince us, that the whole extraordinary expenditure of the war was as little called for by necessity as by any views of advantage; that loans did not even relieve the distresses of the moment; that all the enormous transfer of property which has taken place, did not even shift off the payment of a debt to a more convenient time; that the new proprietors have never paid a shilling of the purchase money; that all their capital they have received as a pure and unconditional gift.

Whoever on the principles of modern political economy examines the history of every national debt, the circumstances under which it has been created, and the manner

in which it has grown, cannot but be forcibly struck with
some strange inconsistencies. The conclusions are always
at variance with the principles. Nothing ever happens as
we are taught to expect it. Peace is supposed to be the
time when capital increases with most rapidity; war is
always looked on as destructive of its growth. Yet it is
always at the breaking out of hostilities, when the hoards
of peace are yet entire, when capital is looking in vain for
employment, that a government finds the greatest difficulty
in making a loan. The more it spends, the more it is supposed to have wasted the national resources, the more easily
it borrows. Its credit rises with its extravagance. The
means of the nation grow the fastest which are destroyed
with most rapidity. What was impossible to the wealth of a
people, becomes easy to their poverty. In the last year of
the last war, after all the exhaustion of twenty years of
boundless extravagance, sixty millions were borrowed with
greater ease than six in the first. Whatever the government wanted was always found; the means of the lender
grew in exact proportion to the borrower's wants. To un-
ravel this mystery, so puzzling to science, will not be difficult to common sense. If, instead of spinning theories,
we attend to facts, we shall see that the expenditure
always preceded the loan; that the nation in borrowing only
changed the description of debts which had been already
contracted ; that the sum borrowed did not on an average
exceed one third of what was spent ; that whenever, as in
the year 1797, it was attempted to exceed this proportion,
great distress was immediately felt by the monied men—that
when, as in that year, the contractors were called on to advance more than their profits, they were only enabled to do
it by persuading the bank to exchange its bullion for their
anticipation of future gains, an exchange which caused the
failure of that establishment ; that the price of every
article for the service of the government was greatly enhanced ; that enormous fortunes were made by all those

who in any way were concerned in supplying its wants. If we weigh all these circumstances carefully, we are irresistibly brought to the conclusion, that the real expenses of the war were, as they must always be, really defrayed by the funds raised from taxes, and that the stock created went only to satisfy the gains of the contractors, and the jobs and peculation which so profusely attended the expense of the war. We shall be forced to conclude, what indeed reasoning would equally lead us to expect that they were only imaginary debts, that were or could be satisfied with an imaginary payment.

It does not require to be proved, that nothing can be consumed but what is already in existence ; armies cannot be fed with corn that is yet to be sown, nor can fleets be victualled with provisions that will only exist hereafter. This, which would be really to anticipate future income, is impossible. Here the skill of the financier entirely fails. His spells are all powerful to change the destination of actual things, but those which shall only come into being in future times will not obey his call. But as whatever is produced must already be income to somebody, and as income derives all its value from expenditure, the expenditure of the whole society must ever be equal to its whole income, it must consume all that is produced. To prevent the waste which would otherwise arise from the perishable nature of all commodities, it is the constant business of society, it is the very principle on which it is constructed, to prevent useless production, by converting the industry which is not required for production, into the industry which lives by aiding consumption, to employ in the luxuries of life those who are not needed for its support. If, however, nothing exist in a country but what is required for its regular and ordinary consumption, it is only from this fund that the waste and expenses of a war can be supported. Individual luxury must give way to this luxury of the nation. The consumption of every people is always

in proportion to its numbers. Lessen the number of consumers, and less will be required for their consumption.
Every man added to the army is one taken from the civil
society of the nation. Those who are called to fight the
battles of their country only consume what would otherwise
have gone to their maintenance in some other situation.
They who now are fed by the state are no longer fed by individuals. That portion of the surplus revenue of the nation,
which is now demanded for national purposes, as it no longer
forms income to individuals, is no longer employed in administering to luxury. As there is less demand for the
industry of consumption, when the means of paying for it
are less, there are so many more people left free to follow
the trade of soldiers., Thus it is that war makes no waste
of a nation's substance, it only gives a new direction to its
employment. What the state takes, individuals lose. The
loss in the one case being exactly equal to the gain in the
other, those who are no longer able to obtain a livelihood
in administering to the luxury of their countrymen, find it
again in serving their vengeance. As every expense,
whether of a state or of individuals, ultimately resolves
itself into the maintenance of men, the same expense will
always maintain the same number of men, for the rich only
consume more than the poor, by hiring others to assist in
their consumption. Soldiers, whose diet is usually spare,
cannot consume more than they would have consumed in any
other condition ; and the diminution of the means of individuals which compels them to take service, as it affords an
equal income to the state, offers the means of supporting all
those whom it drives from private employment. The
growth of luxury, so remarkable in England during the war,
does not invalidate this argument. It was confined to the
upper classes, to those who were benefited by the blun-
ders of our financiers, and they form but a small part of the
nation. The middling and lower classes were robbed of
almost every comfort. The labourer was compelled to do

more work to obtain a more scanty subsistence. He lost, in
reality, one third of his income. What was taken from him
formed a fund fully equal to the maintenance of five-
hundred thousand soldiers, and his increased exertions, by
diminishing the number of those who were required for the
maintenance of the nation, set free that number to be employed for other purposes.

If the events which have passed in our own country could
in any way throw a doubt on these doctrines, the experience
of other countries would amply confirm their accuracy.
France and the other nations of the Continent were not less
deeply engaged in the late war than England ; they did not
embattle a smaller amount of their population ; the battles
they fought were not less numerous or less bloody : their exertions out of all proportion greater, were made without the
assistance of credit. Relying on their own resources, they
raised no loans, they borrowed nothing from posterity ; and
at the end of the war, their exertions and their sufferings,
their losses and their confiscations, had caused no diminution
of their means. If when peace restored our intercourse with
the Continent, we discovered none of the splendour of fictitious riches, there was none of the misery they cause.
Equally ignorant of the extremes of wealth and poverty,
the people was every where comfortable and contented.
England alone, who had kept all her resources entire, who,
carrying on the war by the contributions of future generations, was adding every day to her riches, shewed symptoms
of exhaustion. Germany, so often plundered, missed none
of her comforts ; the loss of her capital had not impaired
her industry. France, though subdued, was cheerful and
happy. It was only in England that the cry of misery was
heard to drown the acclamations of victory.

To a people who for so long a period have been revelling
in the riot and gallantry of expenditure, who like all spend-
thrifts have accustomed themselves to glory in their extra-

vagance and to consider frugality as the virtue of narrow
souls, it may be somewhat mortifying to learn that of the
loans which have so often been dinned in our ears as proofs
of the exhaustless wealth of Great Britain, not one shilling
has ever really been paid by those who claim to be the creditors of the country; that the enormous debt which presses
so heavily on our shoulders is not composed of the hard
earnings of industry generously subscribing for the defence
of its household gods; that it has not grown from the
devotion of patriotism, sacrificing every private comfort to
the public good; but that it is a bloated and putrid mass of
corruption wholly made up of fraud, of peculation, and of
jobs. The nation has run the career of every thoughtless
spendthrift; she has borrowed her own money at usurious
interest; after having paid the full value of every thing
she has received, she still finds herself loaded with a heavy
debt of extortion; her tradesmen, like his, have found in
their unearned profits, in their fraudulent gains, the means
of their usurious loans. They have advanced nothing
which they had not first stolen; what they have lent was
but the upbraidings of their conscience.

The sinking fund, that ingenious delusion which proposes
to discharge debts with borrowed money, which increases its
loans that it may pay them with more ease, has contributed
not a little to the amount of our embarrassments. The intri-
cacy which it introduced into all our financial operations disguised their real bearings even from those who were supposed
to have their direction. The unnecessary amount of our loans
gave them an air of reality; they were too bulky to seem
the creatures of the imagination. It was difficult to persuade men that forty millions were raised, year after year,
without something being advanced in payment of it; that
all this mighty creation was but enough to satisfy the
frauds of contractors and the peculation of jobbers. The
sum seemed too vast for all the powers of malversation. Cor-

ruption itself would have stood aghast, had it appeared in its naked form, had it shewed itself in all its undisguised deformity. But the mystery of the sinking-fund threw a haze over the whole transaction. Between what was borrowed from necessity, and what was borrowed for amusement, between loans that were to increase the debt, and loans that were to pay it off, there was so much confusion, that the clearest sight could see nothing with distinctness. Interest and compound interest, debt and redemption, danced before men's eyes in such perpetual succession; there was such a phantasmagoria of consols and navy, of debentures and exchequer bills, of capital without interest and interest without capital, that the strongest understanding was bewildered. Men shrunk from the inquiry in despair.

But time, which brings all things to light, has enabled us to discover the true nature of all these fantastical operations, to fathom this sink of iniquity and corruption. Taking for our guide an article in a late Edinburgh Review, which has shewn from authorities which cannot be disputed, that of the money raised by the sale of 900 millions of stock created during the war only 114 millions were of real use to the state, that it was the whole of the expense which was not in fact raised by the taxes, it will not be impossible to shew what was in truth the employment of the whole. Of the 900 millions of stock created there was nominally received about 600 millions; but as 390 millions were for the purposes of the sinking fund, the debt really contracted was 400 millions, for which 600 millions of stock was created. Allowing that of this sum 114 millions were really advanced to the state, though it will appear presently that this has no better claims to be considered as a debt than the remainder, it will be shewn that the rest of this enormous sum, amounting to nearly 300 millions, has been wasted in profits to loan contractors, in the machinery of the sinking fund, in the conversion of exchequer and navy bills, and in the compound interest of money which has never been advanced. Incredible as it may seem, the fact cannot be called in question. We are now burthened with a perpetual payment of twenty millions a year to avoid an annual payment of six millions during the war. Such are the happy effects of our financial wisdom, such the advantage of borrowing of posterity, that though we have already discharged the real debt with interest, the claims of our creditors are not in the least diminished. The present generation will pay what they have borrowed more than twice over, and will leave the debt unimpaired to posterity.

It is not possible to follow in detail all the complex transactions of twenty years of war and extravagance, nor to shew in each particular instance what has been the amount of waste and malversation ; but the following statement, without pretending to minute accuracy, which in such cases is only affectation and pedantry, will be sufficient to convince by figures, those on whom reasoning will make no impression, that nothing has been asserted that cannot be proved. The 400 millions which the war added to the national debt is made up of these sums :

The sum of which the state is supposed to
    have had really the use, being the difference
    between the expenditure and the amount
    raised by taxes during the war,   . . .   114,000,000
Compound interest on this sum, 13 years, at
    $5\frac{1}{4}$ per cent. per an. being the average rate
    of interest at which loans were made, . . 108,300,000
Loss by the sinking fund, being the difference
    between the price at which the stock was
    created and redeemed, ...   14,300,000
Compound interest as above, ...   13,600,000
Profit of the loan contractors. As it appears
    that the sinking fund on an average bought
    stock at $7\frac{1}{2}$ per cent. higher than the con-

tract price, and as their purchases were
constant and regular, this may fairly be
assumed as the rate of the contractors'
profit. As the stock created amounted to
900 millions, their profit at 7½ per cent.
will have been 67,500,000
Compound interest as above, ... 63,750,000
Loss on funding of navy and exchequer bills,
and other similar operations, supposed to
amount to 9,000,000
Compound interest as above, ... 8,550,000

Total, . £ 399,000,000

But this is far too favourable a view of our financial
operations. It only shews the direct and immediate loss
which proceeded from the adoption of the funding system;
the differences between the price paid to the state by the
contractors for stock, and the price at which they again
sold it to those whose profits made out of supplies to the
state required to be realized in some shape or other. In
allowing the sum of 114 millions to have been actually advanced to the state, we overlook entirely the indirect but
most important consequences of the funding system; the
waste and extravagance which the apparent facility of procuring money introduced into every branch of the public
service: we suppose that every expense was conducted with
all possible economy, that nothing was ever charged to
government beyond its real value, that there was no peculation, no jobs, no extravagant profits, no half-pay given
to men who had never seen an enemy, no pensions conferred
on others who had never done any service. But though a
minister who made this assertion might be listened to with
attention, and might be cheered by all his dependents, it would
gain no credit even within the walls of the House of Commons, too many of whose members could in their own persons

vouch for its inaccuracy, and it every where else would be laughed at. There is not a man whose own observation has not convinced him of its want of truth. Few indeed are they who have not had an opportunity of seeing with what waste and extravagance every branch of the public service was conducted, what prodigality there was in the whole war expenditure. Jobs and peculation were rank in every department, and what corruption deigned to spare folly threw to the dogs. Transports were hired on such terms as to reimburse the owners their purchase money in a single year. The bills of the commissariat in Spain were sold at rates which insured the purchasers an immediate profit of 30 per cent. There was not a man who could in any way hook himself on to the national expenditure, who, in spite of all his vulgar luxury, did not acquire a princely fortune. The display of upstart wealth which assails us on every side, the men of many millions, whose footsteps none can trace in the paths of regular commerce, may assure us that frugality was not the favourite virtue of the late war. The outgoings of the state, during the continuance of hostilities, exceeded one thousand millions exclusive of the interest of the national debt. On this sum 114 millions is little more than 10 per cent. But if $7\frac{1}{2}$ per cent. was the profit on the loans which were openly contracted, it cannot be doubted that in the furnishing of supplies to government, where there was much less competition and much more mystery, where the secret and ill-understood nature of the profits tempted fewer rivals and admitted more readily of combination, the gains were out of all proportion greater: and we shall be forced to believe that the 114 millions which we have supposed to have been really advanced to the state, were only a small part of the gains which fraud and cunning made out of their dealings with government.

In this statement nothing has been allowed for the additional expense caused by the depreciation of the currency; an event intimately connected with the funding system, and which is entirely attributable to the scheme of borrowing from posterity. How much this tampering with paper added to our expenses it is difficult to compute with any accuracy; that its effect was enormous cannot be doubted, when it is considered that during the four first years of the war, when we maintained an army on the continent, and when most expensive armaments were fitted out for that most expensive theatre of war the West Indies, the annual expenditure exclusive of the interest of the debt, hardly amounted to 20 millions, in the four last years of the war the same annual expenditure exceeded 75 millions. The difference is too great to be accounted for by any difference in the amount of our exertions. Much of it must have been the immediate effect of the depreciation which enhanced the price of every article of consumption, and which probably added 300 millions to our expenditure. But this was the least evil it brought in its train. Its real mischief was the facility it gave to the career of extravagance, the aid it lent to delusion, by creating a persuasion that the prosperity of the country and its revenue were every day growing; that war was but adding to the wealth of the nation. If the nation had wholly consisted of jobbers and contractors, of placemen and pensioners, the assertion would have been true; but the wealth of these men caused the poverty of all other classes. Their splendour was raised on the misery of the people.

The benefits of the Funding System, the advantages of borrowing from posterity, are now fairly before us. They increased our expense at least fifteen millions annually during the war, and they have added twenty millions a year for ever to our burthens. The millions we have since paid have taken nothing from our debt; they are indeed past and gone, but other millions succeed them in interminable procession to the end of time. For what has all this havoc been made in property, since it strengthened not our hand in war, since it gave us no assistance in the hour of battle? Nothing we have seen was ever lent to the state but the unreasonable profits which had already been made out of it, and which, as they represented no property, could in no other way be realized. As the whole expense of the war was in reality defrayed by the amount of taxes yearly raised, if there had been no jobs, no peculation, no extravagant profits to those who had dealings with government, there could have been no loans, and there would have been no need of them; and it may be added, had there been no loans, there must have been fewer jobs and less peculation. Imaginary claims could never have been allowed, if they had not been content with an imaginary payment.

If we had indeed borrowed from posterity, if the debt we have acknowledged had been any thing but imaginary, it must have diminished the means of those who had contributed to it. If it had arisen from extraordinary consumption, its effects must have been felt in a lessening of the existing property. The great consumption of an army is in articles of food; if its supply had been borrowed from the stores of accumulation, its effects must have been seen in our flocks and our herds, in our barns and our granaries. Years of peace would have been required to repair the ravages of war. But during this period of waste and extravagance, whose supposed extraordinary consumption has loaded us with so much debt, our means of subsistence were continually increasing; they grew in exact proportion to the growth of our numbers. At the end of the war, they were found to bear as large a proportion to a population of twelve millions as they bore at the beginning to one of eight millions. As the people had increased one half in number, its produce had increased one half in its amount. Since it is consumption which gives value to production, this must ever be the case. Whilst corn is grown and cattle are bred not for amusement, but for profit, the stock of every country will always be regulated by its wants. The complaint of overproduction which issued from every mouth at the return of peace was not the cry of an exhausted and impoverished people. The great body of the nation was indeed suffering, but it was not from want of the means of subsistence, they were abundant; but because the idle classes had grown out of proportion to the industrious; because the payments to the new creditors of the state, which had hitherto only been made in promises, by new borrowings and new creations of stock, were now to be discharged by giving them a share in the earnings of each man's industry, by transferring to them a large portion of the property of the country. The pressure was great as long as it was attempted to endow the new property at the expense of the already overburdened industry of the country; it ceased as soon as the old gentry, by reducing their rents, had in reality given up one third of their property to form the endowment of their newly-created brethren. The gentry indeed then in their turn felt distress, for the increase in the capital of the nation had brought no addition to its income.

If the wealth of a country be consumed almost in the moment of creation, if destruction always follow close in the footsteps of production, it will naturally be asked how nations ever emerge from that state of penury and destitution which is the lot of every infant community? How plenty succeeds to famine? How comforts and luxury grow where all was squalid poverty? If nothing can be saved, their condition can never alter, their original wretchedness must be without hope and without remedy. Yet the woods and the marshes, the bogs and the glens, among which the few miserable natives of Britain sought a scanty and precarious subsistence, when the ambition of Cæsar first made their existence known to the rest of the world, have long since given way to more cheerful scenes. Cultivation has be-

stowed a new face on the desert. The richest crops now
cover lands whose severest duty was the growth of weeds.
The lowing of the ox, the bleating of the sheep, now glad-
den the plains which then shuddered at the howling of
wolves.   The lazy river no longer wastes its powers
among swamps, but, directed by the hand of industry, its
waters become at once the ornament of the country and the
instrument of its commerce. The deity of the stream, then
weary of beholding only mallards, and pollards, and reeds,
and rats, and widgeons, now rejoices to see reflected in his
waves the pride of populous cities, with their spires, and
their domes, and their towers, and all the glorious handy-
work of civilization. The lowest peasant, hard as is his
condition, probably enjoys more real comforts than ever
surrounded the regal pomp of Caradoc or Cassibelaun.
There is not a citizen whose humble enjoyments might not
excite the envy of their conquerors, the mighty masters of
the world. What power has brought about this happy
change ?   Which is the beneficent deity to whom we are
indebted for all the comforts with which we are now surrounded ? Whose is the temple where we must offer up
our thanks and make known our gratitude?

The political economist who has learnt to troll his bead-
roll will find no difficulty in answering the question. As
Dr. Sangrado, undertook to cure all disorders with water,
so with him the word capital is sufficient to account for
every thing. If nations grow populous, it is the effect of
capital.   If they direct their industry to the cultivation
of their fields, it is capital lends them hands. If they delight in war, it is capital that marshals and feeds their
armies. If they seek their livelihood on the waters, it is
capital that provides the means. If they build cities, and
encourage manufactures, it is still the effect of capital.
Such an answer may be quite satisfactory to science ;
it is not equally so to common sense. Whence came the

capital that creates all these prodigies? Adam left none to
his children; though sticking as close to society, though
more hurtful in its consequences, it is not like original sin,
an inheritance derived from our first forefather. Capital,
like all the productions of man, has had a beginning; but
how that which is the result of accumulation could act
before accumulation took place, could be its cause, is a
problem might puzzle even the ingenious author who has
taught us how Prince Vortigern's grand-father stripped a
painted vest from the body of a naked Pict. To such as
him may be left its solution. Genius may triumph
where reason cannot hope to succeed.

It may not, however, be amiss, to suggest to the sovereigns of Europe and their ministers, who are all smit
with the sacred love of capital, just for the good and ad-
vancement of their favourite science, and the elucidation
of its most obscure doctrine, to catch a capitalist, Mr.
Baring or Mr. Rothschild, it matters not which, and trans-
port him to some of the thinly-peopled countries of Austra-
lasia, with all his bills and his bonds, his coupons and his
counters, his gold and his silver. He will there, according
to the system of modern political economy, have full employment for his capital. He may reclaim marshes and
woods, he may make roads, build bridges, dig canals, and
found cities. He may bring the deserts of New Holland
into the same flourishing condition that Great Britain has
been brought into, we are told, by similar means. So advantageous an employment of his wealth might, one
would think, tempt the cupidity of a capitalist, might
almost excite his ambition. To be the creator of a nation,
and its sovereign, its king, and its proprietor, to owe his
exaltation to the gratitude of a people whom he had loaded
with wealth and surrounded with comfort, is indeed a
glorious prize : it is a condition full of envy. Yet we fear
none of these gentlemen will make the voyage so interest-
ing to humanity, without a little gentle compulsion. Prac-

tice has a surer tact than theory. The children of Mammon are wiser in their generation than the children of Light. They may encourage ministers, in the absurdities of political economy, but they will not share in its delusions. They know that capital can only exist in a rich country, that it grows not by encouraging industry, but by appropriating to itself its earnings. They may suspect, and not without reason, that in New Holland their capital would soon be reduced to its true value. The natives would wing their arrows with their parchments, and give their sovereigns and their Napoleons as playthings to their children. In a country where each man's exertions are barely sufficient for his own subsistence, a capitalist would be the most helpless of animals, all his millions would not keep him from starving.

But though capital is ever struggling against the progress of improvement, by turning away to the maintenance of idlers the labours of the industrious, yet the wealth of all countries is continually growing. It would be wilful blindness not to perceive that every part of Europe is fraught with comforts unknown to former times. Accommodations of all kinds are much more abundant ; disease and famine are of much less frequent recurrence. Those epidemical maladies which formerly from time to time swept away half the population of a country, are now never heard of. The most inclement seasons produce nothing worse than scarcity, except where artificial regulations heighten it into famine. Nor is this improvement in the condition of the human race peculiar to one quarter of the globe, it is felt, though perhaps in a slighter degree, in every part of the world. Savages do not escape its influence. The alterations in a nation's institutions, though they appear to take place at particular periods, have always been brought about gradually. They have been preceded by silent and imperceptible changes in their habits, which

force on them new modes of life. In adopting new laws
and manners they are led, not by choice, but necessity.
The hunter must have made some progress in civilization
before he can pass into a shepherd ; his comforts must have
received still greater additions before he will think of tilling
the earth. Towns cannot be built till increased numbers
allow of a more economical employment of labour. Even
manufactures, the triumph of modern genius, which contribute so much to the civilization of a people, are not the
offspring of choice, they owe their origin to necessity : their
peculiar character is always determined by the condition of
the nation which cultivates them. The savage is clothed
with skins ; the same arrow that procures him food, provides him with clothing. It is to the care of man that the
sheep owes the richness of its fleece ; as population grows,
sheep increase and wild beasts become more scarce : wool-
lens then offer the materials of garments. Hemp, flax,
and cotton, and other vegetable productions, gradually succeed, as the claims of wealth, by reducing the condition of
the great body of the people, force them to live more and
more on leguminous and farinaceous substances. As the
quantity of sheep will always depend on the demand for
the butcher, where the people live principally on potatoes,
there will not be wool enough for their clothing, and the
establishment of the cotton manufacture will indicate, not
the wealth, but the poverty of the nation. In every case
the change in the condition of a people, its improvement in
manufactures, and in all the arts of living, may be distinctly
traced to the increase of its numbers. It is the character,
not the amount, of improvement that is determined by the
manner in which property is distributed. Population does
not grow from plenty, but the better employment of labour,
which only a numerous people can adopt, generates abundance. Numbers increase in pretty nearly equal propor-
tions in all times and in all countries ; but the inhabitants

of a thinly-peopled country are always wretched ; they have
nothing but what is absolutely necessary to existence. If
coarse food be abundant, it is only because, neglecting the
comforts and luxuries of life, all their industry is employed
in procuring the means of subsistence, because all toil to
do what, in more civilized countries, is left to the labour
of a few. Though civilization is continually robbing the
labourer of a greater part of his earnings, though every day
the claims of property become more extortionate, yet the
improvement in the application of labour always keeps pace
with the demands on its earnings. If the people of a populous country consume more than those of a thinly-peopled
district, and that they do can hardly be called in question,
since the greater waste and extravagance of the rich will
always more than compensate any diminution in the comforts of the poor, if any such really take place ; it follows
as an incontrovertible proposition that the amount of production in a rich country must be greater in proportion to
its numbers than in the poorer. Where all consume more,
all must have more. Frugality and abstinence are the favourite virtues of mountaineers, the greater abundance of
the plain holds them in less esteem. Ireland may, indeed,
seem an exception to this rule, for the people are numerous
and they are wretched. Yet their misery cannot be ascribed
to the want of land, for one half of this beautiful and fertile
island is yet a wilderness ; it may with more justice be
attributed to the badness of their government, which, plac-
ing all power in the hands of the landlords, sets no bounds
to their extortion. Rents are higher in Ireland than in any
part of the world.

Numbers, then, are the real wealth of a nation, improvement always follows their increase. Without detracting
from the merit of a Watt or an Arkwright, or even from
that of the great Twemlow (for there is as much merit in
adaptation as in discovery, it is the greatest evidence of

talent to know the signs of the times,) inventions are seldom due to the man who brings them forward ; they
arise from the spirit of the age. The principle of the
steam-engine was known long before the state of our population called it into general use. Had not our men grown
faster than our sheep, had there still been wool enough for
our clothing, Arkwright's spinning-jennies would never
have displayed their graceful movements but for the amusement of the curious. Luxury must have added frills to
shirts before Twemlow could think of box-irons. Invention always sleeps where there is no room for its discoveries. In thinly-peopled countries it is almost unknown.
Where population is making great advances, and its strides
are always largest where it is already most abundant, every
day presents new combinations of machinery, calls into
action powers that a few years before none would have
dared to dream of. Chemistry and mechanics have only
been studied with ardour, since society, needing their aid,
has made their knowledge a road to fortune. The application of steam is still in its infancy ; its stupendous powers
are yet but faintly appreciated. With the experience of
the last years before us, who will venture to set limits to
the discoveries which may be suggested by our necessities,
or to say what new elements may not be subdued and made
to minister to the wants of man ?

This elasticity of nature, this constant tendency in every
people to increase its numbers, and to give a more profitable
employment to its industry, this exhaustless capacity of improvement, is the true capital of nations ; thence flows all
their wealth. They who look for any other will surely
meet with disappointment ; they who would find it in accumulation, they who expect present greatness from past
prosperity, are seeking for the living among the dead.
This principle of vitality it is that brings states, with reno-
vated vigour, through all the diseases of bad government.

It is this power of expansion which has so often rescued them, and will yet often save them, from the consequences of their rulers' folly. But for it there is not a country of Europe whose property would not long since have changed hands ; there would not have been left a gentleman who could trace his ancestry beyond the invention of the Funding System ; all the lands must have years ago passed into the possession of the government, to be distributed among the creditors of the state.

The population of every nation of Europe has been rapidly growing, and with its numbers have increased the means of subsisting them. As the only object of production is consumption, as it would otherwise be without motive and without value ; to say that the gross produce of a people always increases in proportion to its numbers, is only to say that two people consume twice as much as one. So self-evident a proposition needs no proof : nothing need be said on this subject. But though much has been written with the view, the manner in which the nett produce of a country increases, that which is left after satisfying the labourers' wants remains yet to be explained. It depends on a principle so closely interwoven in the texture of society as to seem almost a part of our nature ; the disposition in every community to convert whatever can be spared from the earnings of the industrious to the increase of the idle ; to prefer individual luxury to general comfort. Rent then, or the idle man's share of the industrious man's earnings, that part of a nation's produce which is always employed in the maintenance of unproductive industry, increases not simply in proportion to the increase of the gross produce, but in proportion to the increase of that produce multiplied by the increased skill and knowledge with which the industry of a people may be conducted. There is no invention, no improvement in the management of labour, however alien it may appear from agriculture, that does not tend to

increase the amount of rent. If it does not increase the
labourer's power of producing, it may lessen his expense
of living. The machinery which reduces the amount of
labour employed in the manufacture of clothing, as it more
easily satisfies the wants of the industrious, allows of more
being employed in ministering to the idle. If we suppose
a state of society where each man's labour is so ill applied
that it will scarcely maintain himself, there can be no idle
men and no rents, for they who labour having nothing to
spare from their own wants, the idle must starve. So
soon as an improvement takes place in the application of
industry, so soon as the labour of nine people is equal to
the support of ten, one must live in idleness, and rents are
created ; for if all laboured, as the produce would exceed
the means of consumption, the labour employed in its production would be completely thrown away. But this improvement of skill always follows an increase of numbers,
it cannot indeed take place without it. Machinery can
seldom be applied with success to abridge the labours of
an individual ; more time would be lost in its construction
than could be saved by its application. It is only really
useful when it acts on great masses, when a single machine
can assist the labours of thousands. It is accordingly in
the most populous countries where there are most idle men
that it is always most abundant ; it is among the throngs
of idleness that its powers are displayed with most effect.
It is not called into action by a scarcity of men, but by the
facility with which they can be brought to act in masses.
It must create idle men in order to find customers for its
labours.

In the early stages of society, when men have no artificial assistance to their powers of industry, the proportion
of their earnings which can be afforded to rent is exceed-
ingly small; for land, it must be remembered, has no
natural value, it owes all its produce to industry. But

every increase of skill adds to the proportion which can be reserved for rent. Where the labour of nine is required for the maintenance of ten, only one-tenth of the gross produce can be given to rent. Where one man's labour is sufficient for the maintenance of five, four-fifths will go to rent, or the other charges of the state, which can only be provided for out of the surplus produce of industry. The first proportion seems to have prevailed in England at the time of the Conquest, the last is that which actually takes place. As only one-fifth part of the people are now employed in the cultivation of the land, the rest must in reality live on the produce of their industry. As the population of this country is eight times as great as it was at the period of the Conquest, if this rule be true, it should follow that its rentals should be sixty-four times as great as it then was. It will be well to see how far this reasoning is borne out by experience. At and about the period of the Conquest, or at least as early as we have any traces of subsidies, the population of England was calculated at 1,800,000. It may be laid down almost as a certain rule, that the subsistence of every individual, taking all ranks and classes together, is equivalent to the value of half a bushel of wheat per week. The gross produce of England was then at that period equal to 46,000,000 of bushels of wheat, worth, at 1s. 3d. per bushel of the money of that time, about 2,900,000l., and we learn from the amount of a subsidy that the rental of England, including tithes and every description of property, could not then have exceeded 300,000l., or 900,000l. of the present money. If we adopt the same mode of calculation, we shall find the gross produce of the country to be at present'equal to 360,000,000 of bushels, worth, at 6s. 8d. per bushel, 120,000,000l. ; and the amount of rent, 25,000,000; tithes, 8,000,000 ; county rates, 3,000,000; and taxes, including the expense of collecting them, 60,000,000; making a total of 96,000.000.—

Rent then, for under this name we must include whatever
goes to the maintenance of idle men, and the support of
unproductive industry; of that industry, which, occupied
with the embellishment of society, lives but by the labour
of others, has increased more than one-hundred times,
whilst population has only increased eight times. But
a part of this increase must be rejected; though it may
make a figure in statistics, its existence is wholly imaginary. It arises, not from any addition to the quantity produced, but from the artificial price which our laws have
imposed on corn. If we value wheat at 4s. 6d. per bushel,
the average price it bears thoughout the continent of
Europe, and make some small allowance for the increased
share of subsistence which would then fall to the labourer,
we shall find the gross produce of the country amounting to
81,000,000! and the rent to 62,000,000! being sixty-eight
times as much as it was in the time of the Conqueror.
This is not a nominal improvement in the condition of the
landholder, proceeding merely from a difference in the de-
nomination of money, and met by a correspondent increase
of expenditure; it is a real substantial increase in his
means of living. What, in the mean time, has been the
condition of the labourer? Whilst his exertions have
loaded his landlord with wealth; they have been almost
without benefit to himself: his work is not better paid
than it was; all the discoveries of genius, all the advantages derived from the sub-division of labour, have been not
for him but for his master.

This inquiry might be pursued through every period of
our history, and everywhere the results would be the same:
rent uniformly increasing more rapidly than production; the
processes of labour, as they were conducted with more skill,
becoming continually more beneficial; everywhere the numbers of those who were employed in the industry of consumption, in the industry connected with and dependant on

expense, growing faster than those to whose labours a nation owes its existence. But though the materials of such an inquiry are very scanty, to follow the subject into all its details, important as they are, would extend these pages beyond their proper bounds. It will be sufficient to bring before the reader one more example, drawn from a period of our history when abundance of documents leaves nothing to be supplied by conjecture. At the time the land-tax was first imposed, the population of England was 5,500,000. At the rate of a weekly allowance of half a bushel of wheat per head, the gross produce of the country must have been equal to 143 millions of bushels of wheat, worth at four shillings per bushel 28,600,000*l.* As the expense of cultivation was then one-third of the produce, there remained 19,000,000*l.* for the nett produce, or the idle man's share. Rent accordingly amounted to 10,000,000*l.*—Tithes to 2,000,000*l.*—Taxes, including the expense of collecting them, to 6,000,000*l.*—County rates and other local charges probably absorbed the remainder. Even in the short period that has since elapsed, the share of property in the gross produce of the country has advanced from two-thirds to four-fifths, whilst that of industry has sunk from one-third to one-fifth ; so true it is that society turns every improvement but to the increase of idleness.

Much has been said of late years how population increases in a geometrical, whilst subsistence increases in an arithmetical, ratio. It might be said, with more truth, that subsistence increases in a geometrical, whilst the labour employed in its production only increases in an arithmetical, ratio. At the period of the Conquest more than three hundred thousand men were employed to raise food for less than two millions of people. At present more than twelve millions are fed by the labours of five hundred thousand. Twice the quantity of labour produces eight times the quantity of food. But such coincidences are a

very unsure ground-work for reasoning. They render it
more fantastical than solid. The passions of men do not
allow them to act with so much regularity as to enable us
to reduce the affairs of the world to mere mathematical
abstractions. The plans of Providence, though ever tending to their completion, do not always move on a straight
line. Sometimes they seem to yield to the right, sometimes
to bend to the left, as their progress is opposed by the prejudices of men, as they have to encounter their passions
and their imagined interest. The wisdom that never errs
is content to act rather by insinuation than by force. He
to whom all futurity is ever present ; he to whom eternity is but as a moment, is never pressed for time ; he can
wait his occasions. It has often been noticed, as a proof
of the exhaustless variety of nature's works, that no two
leaves of a tree are exactly alike. This exuberance of
fancy is not confined to the material world, it does not display itself only in inanimate objects. The moral world is
not less chequered, nor less curiously fashioned ; it exhi-
bits as great a variety of forms and colours as the natural.
Men and their systems offer endless varieties ; they shew
themselves, under every possible anomaly of figure ; the
tenderest plants are not more liable to be changed by disease and imperfect modes of cultivation ; they do not more
feel the effects of soil and culture. The observer of human
nature does not less than the botanist find perpetually
new subjects of reflection ; he is not less than him puzzled in his classification of the specimens which are offered
to his notice. Though every people of the earth is continually tending to improvement ; though there is probably
not one that may not look with disdain on the condition of
its forefathers, yet the advance of different nations is very
unequal ; they get forward with very different steps, and
seemingly by very different tracks. What to one seems
the height of wisdom, to another appears the extreme of

folly.   One attributes its prosperity to measures which another would consider as the sure forerunners of ruin.   It is
this plasticity of man's nature, this capacity of taking every
form, and prospering equally under all, that render so ha-
zardous the generalizations of political economy.   Men's
experience is so limited, they are so little acquainted with
the inward workings of their neighbour's system, that their
deductions are too often unfounded ; the facts they collect,
being ill understood, only tend to mislead.   The great law
of existence is indeed invariable ; the rule by which the
world is governed is always the same ; general principles
can never err.   It is their application to individual cases
that puzzles our sagacity.   Particular combinations of the
elements ascending through the trunk of a tree under the
name of sap, will we know at the proper season burst
forth in the shape of leaves ; but what it is that gives to
the leaf of the oak its indented form, why that of the
beech is round and glossy, no human sagacity can discover.
In one of the commonest operations of nature, which is
every day being repeated before our eyes, science is wholly
at fault.   Its political lucubrations are not more successful.   Men are not less puzzled when they find that the
same schemes of government applied to different countries
produce very different consequences, whilst the most dissi-
milar systems of rule often end in the same results.   When
they come to apply their general rules some seemingly
trifling circumstance escapes them, and their attempts
prove no less unfortunate than his who obtained of Jupiter
to regulate the seasons on his farm.   The rain which did
good to his turnips spoilt his barley.   It is the same in the
affairs of men ; there are always so many contending principles in action striving and jostling for the mastery ; individual advantage is always so labouring to modify public
good, that what is beneficial to one cannot but be hurtful
to others.   The world is governed by a system of compen-

sations. There is nothing like positive good. The happiness of men under all their different forms of government probably varies but little in amount. The wisest plans are never without inconvenience ; no scheme of government is wholly without its advantages. The regimen that cures one disease often sows the seeds of others ; the laws which correct one abuse often generate others equally mischievous. Nations are indeed always improving their condition, they are ever tending towards perfection ; but their best directed efforts may not hope to attain it. This consummation of all things is the end of their career, the final term of their existence. When the procession arrives at the temple of the gods, the victim without spot is offered on their altars.

The Funding System can claim no exemption from this general law ; it partakes of the mixed character of all earthly things. All its consequences are not evil. Results little anticipated by its inventors, and less dreamt of by those who have given it so large a sway in the affairs of men, have more than redeemed the mischief it has inflicted on society. Nothing can at first sight be more absurd, or seemingly more fraught with ruin, to a nation than the system of funding. Nothing can abstractedly be more foolish than to create a debt for which no value has ever been given ; to raise up from the lowest and most worthless of the people a new set of patricians ; to rob of a large portion of their property the ancient gentry of the land, to whose ancestors the nation owes its renown in arts and arms, and to transfer it to these new fangled hidalgos as a reward for their skill in the arts of fraud and peculation. Such conduct is surely foolish enough ; yet repugnant as it is to all wise and moral feeling it is not without its advantages ; perhaps on the whole the good predominates. If it encourage fraud and meanness ; if it clothe quackery and pretension in the garb of wisdom ; if it turn a whole people into a nation of jobbers ; if it substitute usury for real trade ; if it break down all the prejudices of rank and birth to render money the only distinction among men ; if it make kings to totter on their thrones, by teaching their subjects to calculate what they cost and what they are worth, it checks violence and eradicates the ruder vices ; it gives power to the law and security to the state, by breaking down the too great masses of property, which when too large to be spent with wisdom, often engage their owners in schemes of rash and turbulent ambition ; it strengthens morals by giving a broader basis to public opinion ; it destroys the perpetuity of property, which by withholding its reward from genius lays heavy on the spirit of improvement. It is by a facility in the acquisition of wealth invention is fostered ; when men cannot better their own condition they will not exert themselves to improve that of others.

In the early stages of society, when population is scanty, and each man's labour barely sufficient for his own maintenance, as the amount of property is very small it is necessarily confined to few hands. Under the reign of our Norman kings there cannot have been in England more than ten thousand owners of land. The whole rental of the kingdom divided among this number will assign to each individual an income of 25l. per annum, equal in value to about 150l. at the present time. This income is but small, for the landholders were then the gentry of the country ; they had no other means of livelihood than their lands. Land was not then held as now, as a mere appendage to trades and professions, as an object of amusement and vanity to those who have other ways of getting money. Indeed, when we reflect on the immense tracts of country then held by some of the powerful barons, when we calculate how little the enormity of their possessions left to be owned by inferior proprietors, this average appears small ; and in computing

the landholders at ten thousand, we probably over-rate
their number. To this number, however, the present rental
of Great Britain would give an average income of more
than 9000*l.* per annum. Such fortunes have in them nothing alarming to the state ; but it is quite otherwise when
we turn from the whole to examine its component parts.
Property never has been and never will be divided
equally among its owners. It is when we contemplate individual incomes that the evil shews itself in the strongest
colours. It is when we think what might have been the
wealth now united in one hand, what the power that
must have accompanied its possession, that the mind
startles with affright. Thomas, from the extent of his domains called the great Earl of Lancaster, is said to have
had an income of 30,000*l.* per annum, equivalent to
more than 160,000*l.* of our present money. Had the same
possessions remained undivided, and had no taxes been
imposed to diminish rents, his descendants would now be
in the enjoyment, (if it be possible for an individual to enjoy such a fortune,) of a rental of ten millions sterling.
This is, indeed, an extraordinary instance, there is probably no other example of a subject in this country seized
of such extensive domains. But history tells of many of the
ancient nobility, who like the Nevilles and the Percys,
had from one fourth to one half of this amount, and
whose descendants, but for the operation of taxes, and the
sales, to which the burthen of wars have so frequently compelled the nobility, might now have had revenues of from
two to three millions a year. Indeed few very ancient families are in possession of more than a tenth of what once
was owned by their ancestors. And it is well that it is so.
No state it is evident could be safe where property was so
unequally divided. Such incomes, too great for wisdom to
spend, too great for liberality to dispense, too great for
folly to waste, could only find employment in mischief,

Their owners could be but a curse to their country. The days of Roman wealth and Roman profligacy might be again revived, and a venal senate might, and in all probability would, be found to dispose of the throne to the best bidder, and to sell the kingdom to the owner of a province. To break down such enormous masses of property, to restrain their owners within harmless dimensions, individual folly and extravagance are wholly impotent; they will only yield to national prodigality or to national animosities, to a bill of subsidy or a bill of attainder, to the tax-gatherer or the headsman. Nor must we imagine that these examples of immoderate wealth are confined to ancient times, it is not necessary to go back to the days of the Plantagenets to convince us with what rapidity property increases. It is in our days that it has made the most gigantic strides. The estates which the bounty of his sovereigns lavished on the princely Buckingham brought him an income of 50,000*l.* The same lands after an interval of less than two centuries pay to their owners in rent, and to the government in taxes, little less than 600,000*l.* Nay, there are among our present nobility more than one, who if the country were freed from taxes, would riot in an income of nearly half a million.

What has happened before we may be sure will again happen. The wisest of men has told us there is nothing new under the sun. The events of one age only differ in colouring from those of another. History is but a repetition of the same follies, of the same pretensions and the same disasters. Nothing is changed but the names. The evils from which accident, not wisdom, has saved us may yet befal our children. The tide of population sets in strong on our shores; and the spirit of improvement walks erect on its waters, its influence is felt in every bay and creek of society. Not a day but may boast of some discovery for the abridgment of labour, and the temper of

the times is bent to turn all to the lucre of landlords.
Rents are growing with a rapidity never before witnessed.
Numbers increase so rapidly, improvements in the management of industry succeed each other so quickly, and
both contribute so equally to the increase of rent, that it
swells with a promptitude almost incredible. It jumps at
once from infancy to manhood. Lands that yesterday were
not worth cultivation, to-day render their owners an ample
income. Every renewal of a lease brings with it an increase of payments. Like the giant, whom some necromancer in the *Arabian Nights* had confined in a chest, rent
scarcely breaks from its bonds but it rises to ten times its
former size. This is, indeed, an evil that may excite some
alarm. If population continue to increase at the rate at
which it has increased during the last hundred years ; if
the skill of our handicraftsmen shall produce as many useful inventions as it has hitherto done, if nothing shall be
added to or taken from the national debt, if the government of the country shall be content with its present fund
of patronage, if the gentry of the land will rather receive
their own directly from their tenants than circuitously from
the hand of the minister ; another century will certainly
see every farm in the kingdom returning to its owner five
times as much as it now pays ; and there will again start
up among us fortunes too vast for the enjoyment of their
owners and the safety of the government.

What then are the evils of the funding system, which
can be set in opposition to the good it does in breaking
down the great masses of property, and giving an excite-
ment to all the active spirits of a nation, by holding out
to them a prospect of sharing in the wealth and dignities
which in countries where property is never put in circula-
tion, they may contemplate indeed with awe and reverence,
but never with hope? Like all other things, it is mischievous in its excess. France was drawn into a revolution

by the impatience of her gentry to submit to taxes; when, exhausted by former prodigality, they could no longer supply funds for new jobs. Holland perished as a nation when her taxes, absorbing all the surplus produce of the country, had virtually transferred all its lands to men who felt no interest in the soil. But, used with moderation, the funding system seems a necessary evil, a corrective for greater ills in countries where the law of primogeniture is established, and entails are permitted. It mitigates the narcotic effects of such drowsy institutions; it has perhaps saved England from the lethargy into which Spain has fallen. The fetters on property are as strict in Scotland as in any country in the world, and till the creation of the national debt, her people, now the most enterprising in Europe, were sunk deep in sloth, and pride, and poverty. This change has indeed been ascribed to the fortunes brought from India into Scotland, and the addition they made to the capital of the country; but the capital which Mexico and Peru unceasingly poured into Spain, only increased her poverty, and sunk her deeper in apathy. It will hardly be thought an objection in a country such as England, where the vicissitudes of commerce have accustomed us to revolutions in property, that the old gentry are degraded by the contamination of these money-lenders, whom lucky hits have raised from the slime and filth of Duke's place and the Stock Exchange, to install them in baronial halls, to endow them with the broad acres of ancient families. This is but a passing evil, for which time will easily find a remedy. In a few generations, when its mellowing influence shall have softened the hard and metallic stream which now flows in their veins, the descendants of the Ricardos and the Rothschilds will make as good gentlemen, will shew themselves as perfect in all the lineaments of high birth as the Darcys or the D'Aeths. The origin of almost all great houses is lost in obscurity—they do not all begin with heroes. If the mist were dissipated which shrouds their first steps in darkness, it would be seen that most have owed their beginning to painful industry, to lucky chances, or to daring villany. Their blood has only become pure when they have become great. Shields, and crests, and pedigrees, are never refused to those who have houses, and manors, and parks. The science of blazonry has in no way degenerated from its ancient virtue. It may still, as formerly, boast to be the school of courtesy; modern heralds are not a whit behind their predecessors in civility and good breeding. Even the monsters they keep in their menagerie, softening down their rough natures, have caught the spirit of their calling—their lions and their panthers, their griffins and their tigers, are always ready to come forth and assume every shape; gardant, passant, or couchant, at the bidding of those who hold in their hand the golden talisman of the prophet. The Garter and Clarencieux bear in mind that Adam was the first gentleman, and never refuse coat armour to those of his descendants who bear themselves *rampant* in a field *or*.

Whatever opinions may be entertained of the funding system, however much men may doubt whether its good or evil weighs heaviest in the scale, but one judgment can be formed of sinking funds; they are unqualified evils, they have no virtues to redeem their vices. With many it may seem a sufficient objection to them that they are working a change in all the relations of property. But this is the least of their wrongs. Change is not necessarily an evil, it is inseparable from our condition; it is the great law of nature, from whose observance we cannot escape. All the works of creation are continually assuming new forms: so rapid are their shiftings, that the eye is scarcely fixed in their contemplation when already they appear other than they were. Whatever exists is always

hastening to its end, that by its destruction it may give
birth to new beings.   Folly and presumption can alone
claim for the institutions of man a stability denied to the
works of his Creator.   The puny lord of an hour may toil
and fret, and, forgetting the short span of his existence,
may form schemes of future greatness, but he may be as-
sured that the seeds of decay are always sowed in the
bosom of improvement, that whilst he fondly believes he
is building for eternity, Time stands by to strike with his
withering dart the noblest monuments of human genius,
ere yet they have risen to completion.   Yet, though yield-
ing to his destiny, man may willingly submit to the mild
operation of change, he may feel appalled at the stern aspect of revolution.   The prodigality of the late war has
worked an almost entire alteration in the property of the
country.   The havoc it has made could hardly have been
more extensive if revolution, in her frantic gambols, had
struck at kings, and lords, and bishops, and all the robed
and titled vanities of the world.   New men have intruded
into seats which a thousand years of possession had sanctified to their owners.   The painted walls have spoken in
vain—the threatening aspect of the warrior, the mild sup-
plications of the venerable churchman have been no protection to their descendants ; the widow has been driven
from her home, the orphan, fondly lingering near the
battlements which once marked the greatness of his house,
in vain re-claims the inheritance of his fathers.   One-third
of the property of the country has been handed over to
Jews and usurers, whilst another third has only escaped
from their fangs by the aid of a law, which, artificially
raising the price of bread, has carried misery and famine
into every cottage in the kingdom.   But these sufferings
have been   endured ; nothing can now prevent them.
The   tempest has passed over ; the lightened atmo-
sphere is again gladdening all nature with the feeling of

calm, the trees of the forest are putting forth new shoots,
and the weaker plants, which had been struck down by the
pelting of the storm, are again raising their heads, and
sucking in the fragrant breath of morn.   The industry of
the country and its increasing population are fast rising
superior to the folly of its rulers. Its growing prosperity
has proved too strong for their deeds of ruin. Its strength
is daily increasing, and the burthen which not long since
seemed intolerable to all, will in a few years be scarcely
heeded. The mischiefs of the funding system will be forgotten, the traces of its violence will be obliterated, and
men will only remember that it has created new proprietors, somewhat too rapidly indeed, in proportion to the
increasing property of the kingdom ; that it has prevented
one of the greatest evils which can befal a country, the
concentration of its revenues in too few hands.

   Is this a condition so full of fear that we should look at
it with dread ?   Is this a moment when the changes which
time necessarily brings in his train should be hurried on
by the foolish impatience of men ?   To pay off the national debt is not to place things where they were, it is not
to recall those associations which antiquity had rendered
venerable, it is not to restore the wanderer to his home ;
it is to bring about a revolution in property as complete as
that we have undergone, without any of its alleviating
circumstances ; it is to heap up again, but in new hands,
whose rapacious feelings have not yet been blunted by
enjoyment, those overgrown masses of property, which a
regard for the safety of the state should induce us to break
down : it is to forget that protection is the first duty of a
government to its subjects, to sacrifice the weak to the
strong, to offer up the widow and the fatherless to the
avarice of the rich. It must not be imagined, that in
paying off the national debt we shall reduce the wealth of
those who were made rich by its creation ; that the loss
will fall on those who have enjoyed the gain. To the dealers

in property, to the men who are used to derive advantage
from every fluctuation in a nation's counsels, the new change
will not bring less profit than the old.   Guilt is somewhat
suspicious; the thief is too cunning to be caught with snares ;
whilst the thing is yet the main or unconverted overt,
he dreads a claim of restitution.   He hastens to the first
market-overt, to exchange his ill-gotten pelf for the more
substantial possession of land, and when the hue and cry
is raised, he is the first to join in the pursuit, the loudest
in his exclamations against the rogues who have robbed
him of his rent, and rendered valueless his acres.   Having
defrauded the old proprietor of his estate, he is now ready to
cheat him of its price.   The funded property of the country
is no longer the portion of speculators; it has become
mixed with all the domestic transactions of the nation; it
is the subject matter of settlements and trusts, it is the
support of the widow and the hope of the fatherless; it is
the retreat of hard-earned industry, the refuge of fallen
greatness.   If ever fund was sacred, surely this is.   To destroy it could only enter into the head of a cold-blooded and
wrong-headed political economist, who, shut up in his
closet, lost in abstraction, and bewildered in the confusion of his own ideas, has cast away all sympathy with his
fellow-creatures, and with the frenzied zeal of a madman
is ever eager to pursue his favourite scheme, reckless of the
havoc he is dealing around him, and seeing no way to
possible good but through certain evil.   The statesman
who could adopt such a project would be wholly unfit for
his station.   True wisdom cannot be separated from humanity.   None but a distempered imagination will conceive that the ruin of a part of its members can contribute
to the happiness of a people.

To pay off a debt which a nation has once contracted
is not less wicked than to cancel it.   The two operations differ but in name : they equally consign to beggary all those who have confided in the good faith of

the government. The repayment of such a debt can
never be otherwise than imaginary; as nothing was received by the state when it was created, so nothing will
be given when it is annihilated. The obligations of the
state have a value, because their holders have a rent-
charge on the industry of the country, they share in its
earnings. Relieve industry from this charge, and the national debt will have but an imaginary existence. The
millions in the books of the Bank, as they will represent
nothing, will from unbounded wealth dwindle into waste
paper. But the payment of the national debt implies the
cancelling of the interest. This rent-charge on industry
will have passed into other hands. It may have gone to
increase the comforts of the industrious, but it is more
probable that it will have been seized on to swell the exactions of the landlord. The wealth of these new proprietors
cannot exist but by destroying that of its old proprietors,
the creditors of the country. If an equivalent be given,
them the debt will not have ceased to exist; its name only
will have been changed: it will still be a rent-charge on
the industry of the country. As the earnings of industry
constitute the matter of property, there can be no property
producing income which is not a rent-charge on industry.
It is however not easy to see what equivalent can be given
them. The only payment of their debt which would not
be a mockery of their claims, would be to distribute among
them a portion of the land. If a part of the industry of
the country be diverted from the purposes of consumption
to the acquisition of gold and silver, and these hoards be
applied to the payment of the debt, the creditors will, in
fact, receive nothing. They will have exchanged their
claim on living industry for one on an industry that no
longer exists, their share in present and future things for
a share in past. As the gold and silver thus accumulated
will be beyond the wants of society, it will be entirely

without value; instead of being a treasure, it will only be an incumbrance. We shall give to our creditors the representative of wealth whilst we keep to ourselves its reality.

But though the injustice of such a scheme, and its impracticability are sufficiently apparent, when viewed altogether, when all its consequences are at once set before our eyes, yet men will delude themselves into the belief that the result will be different, if brought about by degrees, they persuade themselves that all the parts will produce something different from the whole. It is this fallacy which constitutes the delusion of sinking funds. As they are supposed to act gradually, it is imagined they may do so without changing any of the existing relations of society. But if they do not, they do nothing. Their mischief must be as extensive as their power. A sinking fund can only be created by subtracting a part of the produce of the country from its present owners to bestow it on others. As production has no value but what it derives from consumption, as income exists but for expenditure, the whole consumption of a country must ever be equal to all its produce; it never can be more, and it never can be less. The consumption of all the produce of a country requires the expenditure of its whole revenue; and the employment of its revenue can only happen by the consumption of all its produce. Consumption and production are equal powers, which are continually neutralizing each other.

If a nation do not adopt the useless plan of accumulating gold and silver, a sinking fund can only act by giving to the creditors of the state, instead of a perpetual rentcharge on the industry of the country, something which has no value but for immediate consumption, something which at the end of the year will already have ceased to exist. It compels the stockholder to be a spendthrift, unless he can find some-land owner to ruin himself in his stead. If the

stockholder, or somebody for him, do not in addition to
his ordinary income spend the whole amount of the sinking
fund, there must be a part of the revenue of the country
which will not be spent, and of course there will be a part
of the produce which will want a consumer. Any other
supposition must be a contradiction in terms, for it would
imply that the income of a country can exceed its whole
produce ; that all the produce from whence the income is
derived can be consumed whilst a part of the income is
laid by; that revenue can exist independent of the matter
which constitutes its being ; that there can be an accident
without a subject. It would suppose that there is income which arises out of nothing, whilst there is produce
which affords income to nobody.

These conclusions do not rest solely on theory : though
it is not much in the habits of governments to afford examples of economy, yet reasoning here may call in the aid
of experience : all its suppositions have been realized.
Shortly after the last peace the government endeavoured to
raise the public revenue beyond the expenses of the state, and
all the consequences here pointed out immediately ensued.
The distress which has been ascribed to a transition from
a state of war to that of peace was the effect of this blun-
der in finance. The people seemed to be starving in the
midst of plenty. One half of the nation was groaning
under the load of superabundance, whilst the other half
was suffering all the misery of famine. All the bonds
of society were broken up ; all men's opinions were turned
adrift. The wildest paradoxes gained belief ; men almost
persuaded themselves that plenty could be the cause of
evil, that to abundance they owed all their wretchedness.
The farmer, indeed, could not sell his corn, for there was
none to buy it. The consumer could not purchase ; for
what should have constituted his income was stopped in
its passage through the exchequer. As there was a part
of the income of the country which formed revenue to

nobody, there was a part of its produce which could find no consumer. The only year in which this country ever saw any considerable reduction of the national debt was a year of unexampled and unaccountable distress. The attempt to sever revenue from consumption ended in universal wretchedness. Ireland has since repeated the dreadful lesson for the instruction of statesmen. That ill-fated country, where property is every thing and men nothing, witnessed the most portentous phenomenon that ever brought shame on afflicted humanity. She saw her people dying of hunger without any rise in the price of corn. The starving natives had no means of purchasing it; for, as the landlord's interests were first to be cared for, he took the whole of the scanty crop, all the people's means of subsistence, and sent it to England to be sold in payment of rent. These things have happened in a Christian country. They have called forth no remonstrances from a well-paid clergy. Are such the precepts of the gospel?

A consideration of these circumstances may account to the late Chancellor of the Exchequer for the failure of his attempt to reduce the national debt; an event which must so often have puzzled his philosophy. He exhausted all the resources of stock-jobbing. Brokers looked with wonder and envy at the variety of his conceptions, and the subtilty of his stratagems. His tactics seemed inexhaustible. He attacked the debt on every side and in every shape; he made his approaches by every possible avenue; he manœuvred in every way to get round it; he coaxed and he threatened, he caressed and he cajoled, he tried to persuade and he strove to intimidate. But all his contrivances and all his blandishments were thrown away: the debt was obstinate, and would not yield; and eight years of peace and superabundant revenue brought no diminution of its amount. If his successor has been more fortunate, if he can really shew debt paid off, he 'owes his success to the invention of the dead weight, which allows him to create with one hand as much debt as he destroys with the other. The financial relations of society thus remain unaltered : every thing goes on as usual, except that a part of the nation's income is wasted in keeping up the clumsy and antagonistic machinery of these contending principles.

A national debt may, indeed, be reduced, if not in its capital, at least in its interest; if not in name it may yield in reality. As there is no natural proportion between capital and interest, as money has no value but what it derives from the will of society, its relations must always give way to the expression of that will. As the seller always receives as much money as the buyer pays, the plenty or scarcity of money must be merely matter of opinion, and the rate of interest must depend on the will of speculators. As they live by change, they dread nothing so much as stability. It is their interest, when no loans are making, that the value of stock should be continually rising : it is the only game they can play with success against the other classes of society. It is, therefore, always easy for the minister who holds the law in his hand, and who has so many ways of influencing the opinion of monied men, to make the rate of interest what he will. He has only to practise some of those tricking contrivances which the underlings of finance mistake for the pride of political wisdom : but the policy of such conduct is as questionable as its justice. To reduce the interest of the debt is not less a transfer of property than to destroy it. Disguise it under what name you will, to reduce their interest, as it must always be done against their will, is not less a robbery on the widow and the orphan than to cancel their claim ; it differs but in measure. It is to take from them all that renders their property valuable. This preserving the name and destroying the reality, this keeping entire the capital and lowering the interest, savours a good deal too much of the morality of Figaro, who tells his creditor that he will never think of denying his debt, provided he is never called on to pay it; it is unworthy of a nation. As it tends to bring property into fewer hands, it is contrary to its interests.

Since a sinking fund cannot lessen consumption, without diminishing production, it cannot restore the exhausted vigour of a nation; that must be the work of time. Its merits, therefore, may be summed up in a few words: it destroys present enjoyment that it may create future misery; it makes one part of the nation unhappy now, that it may make another wretched hereafter.

They are melancholy reflections, and humbling to the pride of human nature, that rise in the mind when it turns back to contemplate the history of the last thirty years. The passages of that eventful period display in the liveliest colours the weakness of man and the nullity of his wisdom. For twenty years the rulers of this country bent themselves with unwearied assiduity to spread the flames of war from one end of the world to the other. The globe was shaken to its centre; the existence of all created things seemed at stake; not a nation that they did not subsidize or attack, not a people whom they did not strive to entice or to force into the vortex of their mad ambition. Europe was torn by contention; the strength of Asia was poured out on Africa; whilst the sable sons of the Niger were embattled to keep down the rising of America. Every sea was tinged with the blood of Englishmen; not a land but their bones are whitening on its plains. And what has been the issue of all these machinations and contrivances, of all this havoc and bloodshed, of this taxation and squandering, of this waste of treasure and of life? An age of dissentions and animosities, of heart-rendings and blood-sheddings, has left the world pretty much where it found it. It has achieved no higher adventure than the turning a few Jews into gentlemen, and a few blockheads into political economists.

There may be countries where the condition of the people is so easy, where the exactions of property are so moderate, that taxes may be required to subdue the exuberance of the soil, and to produce a tilth fit for the culture of society. But surely England is not among them: it cannot be necessary that her ministers and her parliament should amuse themselves with the sorry farce of a sinking-fund, which, if its produce be not wholly wasted, can only transfer property from one class of persons to another, in order to quicken the faculties and to call out the energies of Englishmen. What may be sport to their rulers is suffering to the people. Kept for ever on the rack of exertion they know no repose; the urgency of their present wants leaves them no time to think of the future. Toiling unceasingly in the tread-mill of life, with all they can grasp for ever slipping from their hold, if fainting under their labour, they make one false step, they fall never to rise again. The ministers of the law, like the devils in Dante's Inferno, stand by to catch the unfortunate wretches, whom weakness has driven to the shore, and to plunge them in a fire ten times hotter than that they have left. They who have never turned their mind to the subject, and it is one from which it shrinks with alarm, can little imagine how completely the wants of the treasury have debauched the law, and blotted out from the minds, not of the people only, but of the judges, the broad and eternal distinctions of justice and morality. It is a strange perversion of intellect, an utter abandonment of principle that can look on and punish, as atrocious crimes, mere offences against the revenue. It is to cast the sword of the law into the scale of justice. The law thus administered, becomes a snare for the people, a temptation to wickedness. There is hardly a man, who answers with his life for his

transgressions, that might not say, " But for the law, I had
not known sin. The making forbidden offences more cri-
minal than those which nature abhors, has been my ruin.
If the law had not visited with undue severity, the act,
harmless in itself, of having in my possession a cask of spirits or a pound of tea, I had never fled my home, and become an outlaw and a murderer." And these things are to
be endured for the sake of a useless sinking fund. The
people are to be starved, and their morals corrupted, that
the minister may tell parliament that the finances of the
country are flourishing. The repeal of the five millions of
taxes, which are now consecrated to the upholding of the
sinking-fund, would, by their abolition, so much increase
the produce of other branches of the revenue, as to admit
of lowering all the duties on consumption. Smuggling
would then no more be heard of, and with their occasion,
might be abrogated the odious and bloody laws which now
fence round the collection of the revenue. It is a dreadful thing that in a Christian country, and one that is ever
ready to vaunt its religion, the interests of morality
should be sacrificed to trifling and mistaken considerations
of revenue. The repeal of one tax would, in its consequence, do more good to the morals of the people than the
establishment of a hundred Bible Societies, or the building of five hundred new churches. If idleness be the
parent of vice, among the rich, it is misery which generates it among the poor. Honesty has little hold on men
to whom it cannot procure the means of living. They
have much to answer for, who by excess of taxation break
down the spirit of a nation, and corrupt its morals.
The gold which is wrung from the wretchedness of a
people, is stained with blood, and robbery, and murder,
and all the crimes its exaction drives men to commit.

But there are evils still worse than taxation, and England is doomed to know them. It is hardly possible to con-

ceive a measure so fraught with mischief to a nation, so full of hatred and discord, as a law which shall persuade men that their interest consists in starving their fellow-creatures, which makes them watch with hope and pleasure for the moment when they may deliver them over to the sufferings of famine. When Satan looked over the earth, and saw how good it was, his cheek, we are told, turned pale with envy at the happiness of man. Had he foreseen the invention of corn-bills, in spite of the malice of his nature, his envy must have given way to pity; had he dreamt of this more insidious engine of murder, he had spared Cain the slaughter of his brother. This contrivance, too atrocious for the Devil, has been left for the wickedness of man to conceive; and England boasts the invention. There is no hope for her people ; their wretchedness must ever arm them with hatred against their rulers as long as this ill-advised law is allowed to disgrace the statute book. It is as impolitic as it is cruel. It has reduced the people to the level of their cattle who drag the plough without any benefit to themselves. In shewing to them that no exertions of their own can better their condition, it teaches them to be idle. They have no motive to be industrious who know that all their earnings will go into the pocket of their masters. They will have no repugnance to derive their maintenance at all times, from the parish, who know that the slightest failure of the crop will compel them to submit to this disgrace. The idle and dissolute are put on the same footing with the industrious ; what is necessary to all, cannot be disreputable to any. If the members of the House of Commons, instead of plotting how they may relieve their estates from the burthen of the poor-rates, would look into the cause of their increase, they would find it in their own avarice. If they will have high rents, they must bear with their consequence. Heavy taxes on consumption have raised the price of subsistence, without raising the wages of labour. Having re-

duced the labourer's earnings to the lowest sum on which
he can subsist, when in health and employ, his maintenance
necessarily falls on his master, when any of the accidents
to which humanity is subject, render him unable to provide
for himself. The labourer, who can lay by nothing from
his own earnings, is as much a slave as if bought with his
master's money, and will not escape the vices of his condition. They who will enjoy the luxury of having slaves,
must bear with the inconvenience of the practice. The
poor, in questions of moral and political economy, generally
reason better than the rich; for their interest never mis-
leads them. They who have nothing, can find no good in
wrong-doing. It is to property alone that systematic injustice can be profitable. The poor man is not so little
observant of what is passing in the world, as not to
know that the seasons are changeable ; he is not so little
versed in the history of past events as not to know,
that from time to time, scarcity will scourge the most fa-
vored lands : he knows that it is the mean employed by Providence to keep up a friendly communication among nations
to bind them together by an interchange of wants and
superfluities. What motive can he have for exertion when
he feels it will be useless to him ? When the corn-bill,
with a malignant spirit worthy of the author of all evil,
aggravating the slightest scarcity into famine, calls on
him for expenses which no savings he can make can ever
hope to meet, it matters not to him that the scarcity is
artificial, that the country is indeed full of corn. He who
out of eight shillings per week must pay fifteen-pence for the
quartern loaf, is suffering the scourge of famine as much
as if there was no bread in the land. He will not save, to
whom the corn-bill has sternly decreed that nothing shall
ever raise him beyond the reach of want. He will not strive
to better his condition, to whom it is but folly to lay up
against the evil day. This odious system must at last

prove injuriosu even to landlords. In breaking down industry you destroy the source of rent. There is no incen-
tive to labour like the hope of reward ; it is a light heart
that best strings the sinews to exertion.

It has been urged in extenuation of the corn-bill, for
no one has been shameless enough to justify it, that the
expense of cultivation being higher in England than in
other countries, it is necessary to protect the farmer against
the competition of foreigners. Never was assertion so
wholly unfounded. It is built on a miserable quibble between the real and nominal expense of things. Because
wages are nominally higher in England than on the continent, it is contended that they are really so. The effect of
the corn bill is brought to show its necessity. Where labour is employed with most skill, as its results must be
most advantageous, it must be in reality the cheapest. The
superiority of English industry is never so manifest as when
it is left entirely without protection. The most flourishing of our manufactures, that of cotton, owes its material
to foreigners, it depends on them chiefly to consume its
produce. By the greater cheapness of labour alone, it is
enabled to return them their own material manufactured
for less than it would cost them to work it up at home.
Our agriculture can boast of not fewer advantages. The
smaller proportion of our people employed in raising food,
is decisive evidence of the cheapness of our husbandry.
That work really costs least which is done by fewest men.
In Russia and Poland, four-fifths of the people are employed
in raising the subsistence of the whole. In England, this
task is performed by one-fifth part of our numbers. But
the real expense of cultivation is that part of the crop
which is consumed in its production. As this in Russia is
four-fifths, and in England only one-fifth, to raise corn in
England really costs only one-fourth of what it costs in
Russia. That it is in fact produced at less expense in

England than in any other country, may be shown from a comparison of rents. As rent is that which remains after paying the expense of cultivation, where that is highest the expense must be least. The quarter of wheat which can afford the landlord three bushels must have cost the farmer less than that out of which he can only pay one. In whatever way we make the calculation, the result is always the same; the surplus is always largest in England. If we look to the industry employed, we shall find that in England each man's labour produces 160 bushels over and above his own consumption. In France, the surplus is not more than 100. In Russia what the labourer can spare from his own wants hardly amounts to forty. In money-rents the disproportion is still greater. In Russia, of whose fertility so much has been said, land on an average, does not produce its owner one shilling per acre. In France, the landlord receives seven shillings. In England, he complains when he only gets twenty-two shillings. If in England the farmer, notwithstanding all the burthen of taxation, can yet pay a rent three times as great as that received in any other country, he must grow his corn cheaper than foreigners. From their competition he needs no protection. He only requires to be defended from the extortion of his landlord. The good of the farmer is indeed only the pretext, the good of the landlord is the real object of the corn-bill; it proposes to increase rent by diminishing the real wages of labour.

This political economy is, in truth, a vile illiberal study: it corrupts the kindliest natures. The English gentleman was once generous, it was his pride to be careless of money, but since he has dabbled in statistics nothing can satisfy his greediness. Like the daughters of the horse-leech, his cry is for ever "Give, give." He would only leave to the other classes of society wherewith to supply what may be needed for his and his children's sobs.

They are his necessities, he will tell us, that compel him
to be griping. Taxes have so much raised his expenses,
that he cannot live as he would do without exacting more
from his tenants. He only asks of them to make up what
the government takes from him. He only desires that a
war, which has transferred one-half of the property of
the country to new owners, should be without injury to
himself. Let him but have a little patience, and time and
the growing population of the country will restore to him
what his own folly has thrown away. In the mean time it
does not seem quite just, that the people who had no share
in the prodigality should alone bear all its burthen. Let not
the gentleman rely on his claims of property, let him
not tell us that the land is his, and that he has a right to
get for it what he can. He should remember that property, which is created for the good of society, incurs
forfeiture, whenever forgetting its tenure, it becomes injurious to its interests. There was a time when the people
of Cornwall looked on it as part of their property to plunder and murder those whom the raging of the elements
had thrown on their shore ; the seaman escaping from
shipwreck, the merchant whose hopes had been baffled by
Providence, were a regular part of their income ; they found
in the distress of their fellow-creatures a remedy for
the barrenness of their soil, something that made up for
the badness of their crops. Unless they robbed these
poor wretches, the produce of their lands could not be
made equal to that of more fertile regions ; their owners
could not vie in expense with their more fortunate neighbours. Time seemed to have given them a vested interest
in their inhumanity ; their claim was sanctified by long
enjoyment, the only real title to all property. If the law
was justified in preventing and punishing such enormities,
has it done right to authorize another more dreadful, as its
inflection is more extensive ? With what face can it forbid

to the half savage Cornish man this old and long-practised method of increasing his revenue, whilst it allows the gentry to aggravate the evils of scarcity, and to plunder and starve their unfortunate countrymen whom Providence, by the inclemency of the seasons, may throw into their hands? What rights can the land-storm give, that the raging of the sea may not equally claim to bestow ? Is the word of the Lord forgotten which says, that wickedness shall never prosper ? Must we wait to learn from our own experience that plunder never turns to profit ? Shall we bring no remedy to this crying iniquity till the poor laws, wringing from the griping hands of the land-owner his gold soiled with the blood and tears of his fellow-creatures, shall have taught him that the suggestions of avarice are as foolish as they are atrocious.

Many yet remember when, towards the close of the last century, the military and financial operations of government had raised the price of provisions so much above the means of the poor, as virtually to create a famine. The people in their distress came to the bar of the House of Commons, crying, " Oh, give us bread, or we die." But the members armed themselves with philosophy ; they told the people to have patience ; that plenty and scarcity were the work of God ; that human legislation could have no influence over them. In a few years the scene was changed. A fall in the price of corn threatened to bring down rents. The gentry lost all their philosophy, their reliance on Providence was shaken, and impiously striving to wrest from the right hand of God the noblest of his attributes, his ounty, they determined, as much as in them lay, that the people should never again know the blessing of plenty.

There may be a tyranny so atrocious that, in the words of Burke, " every man is bound to resist it to the utmost of his power, whenever it shall show its face to the world. It is a crime to bear it when it can be rationally shaken off. Nothing but absolute impotence can justify men in not resisting it to the utmost of their ability." Rome drove out her kings because the chastity of a woman had been violated. England changed her dynasty, because her sovereign chose to worship God in a way different from his people. But what is the form of a mass, what the chastity of a woman, compared with the sufferings of a starving people?

As the only pretext for the corn-bill was taxation, a reduction of taxes would call for its repeal, and again putting the industry of England on an equality with that of other countries, would throw the burthens of society on those who alone enjoy its advantages. The sins of the corn bill are on the head of the Sinking Fund; it must answer for all the misery that flagitious measure may engender.

We have surely persisted long enough in error to satisfy us that we have wandered from the true path, and are gone astray; that in hunting after capital we are only pursuing a phantom. All its promises have ended in disappointment. Instead of showering down plenty on the heads of the people, it has only sunk them deep in wretchedness. It has not added more to the power and splendour of the state than it has to the happiness of individuals. It was a simple age, and not pretending to wealth, that raised the stupendous piles for the worship of God, which towering beyond the daring of modern genius, still look with derision on the puny and paltry buildings with which capital trafficking in religion has studded our streets, as if to mark the poverty of our conceptions and the littleness of our means. When the nation could boast of nothing but the richness of its soil; when its trade was carried on by the capital of Holland, it was great among the powers of Christendom, and Cromwell was able, without borrowing, and with none but national means, to bridle the rising ambition of France, and to set bounds to the unwieldy greatness of Spain. Now, in the fulness of our wealth, when our capital is running over to the uttermost limits of the earth ; when, having drained and exhausted our native industry, it is seeking for new prey in foreign lands, we have heard the humiliating avowal that England's voice is not listened to in Europe ; that her threats have no terrors for the wrong-doer.

It is time to clear away the mist in which the sophistry of political economy has bewildered our understandings. It is time to wake from the dreams of wealth which is to be produced by the encouragement of idleness. God, when he said to man, " Go forth, increase and multiply, by the sweat of thy brow shalt thou live," pointed out to him the true source of the wealth of nations, numbers, and industry. To his own exertions man was to owe every thing. Nature indeed always kept a rich treasury ; her garners were full, but her stores were only for those who, by the proper employment of their faculties, had shewn themselves worthy of her bounty. In order to secure man's obedience to this great law of his existence, that the necessity for his exertions might never relax, that plenty might not encourage sloth, it was decreed by almighty wisdom that all the productions of the earth, every object that could contribute to the sustenance of life, should be of a perishable nature ; that, if not consumed in its right season, it should be wholly useless. Accumulation was thus rendered impossible ; since to save was but to waste. When man, tasting of the tree of knowledge, learnt to double all his faculties, and by a wiser direction of his industry to make the labour of an individual suffice for the maintenance of many, this law, so necessary to his happiness, was not abrogated. He was indeed enabled to increase the means of production, to multiply and render more effectual the instruments of labour ; he might grow rich in new comforts and new luxuries, he might swell the amount of his enjoy-

ments, but to lay by was still beyond his power. The productions of his industry yet retained their perishable nature; whatever he saved disappeared in the moment of
hoarding. In vain the wilderness became, under his hand,
a garden; in vain the heather and the broom gave way to
the richest crops; the work of destruction kept pace with
the labours of production, and what man's consumption
spared vermin devoured. Each returning year saw him
doomed to recommence the labour needful to his existence;
each change of the seasons repeated in his ear the warning
of the apostle, " He that will not labour neither shall he
eat." Man cannot escape from his destiny; his capacity
of producing beyond his wants is given him, not for useless
saving, but for profitable enjoyment; it is bestowed on
him that the care of his subsistence may not for ever bow
him to the earth; but that leisure and reflection may improve him in that higher knowledge to which he shall
ascend by degrees, and which, seizing on it as the birth-
right of the chosen and favoured object of creation, shall in
due time restore him to that communion with his Maker,
from which he fell by listening to the suggestions of the
tempter, who taught him to forfeit happiness for the
mockery and delusion of imaginary wealth, and of vain
knowledge that leads to nothing.

And is this foretaste of heavenly things to be forfeited for
the accumulation of capital? What good has capital ever done
for man? where are we to look for its triumphs? in what part
of the world are to be seen the monuments of its achieve-
ments? It has visited every people in its turn, but so fleet-
ing is its step that it leaves no traces behind; as well might
you hope to track the passage of a ship in the sea. It has
ever followed on the prosperity of a state, and been the
forerunner of its decay. Nations, who by too much forcing
of the idle classes, rise at once to premature wealth and

greatness, sink as rapidly into exhaustion and decrepitude. Their riches never stand the test of time; their capital, when it seems all powerful, when surrounding eyes look with expectant wonder for the miracles it is about to perform, suddenly vanishes from sight, and leaves behind no vestiges of its existence. Theirs is the fate of all those too-daring spirits who, hoping to penetrate the secrets of nature, and by their knowledge to obtain a mastery over her arts, give themselves to unhallowed studies; their power is but delusion. Like the necromancer, they gain no empire over realities; they are but the shadows of forms that obey his call. Like the alchymist, their gold disappears in the very moment of projection; like his, their visions of wealth end in broken retorts. What has their capital done for Tadmos and Palmyra but strew the desert with their ruins? Where are the fields the wealth of Carthage has fertilized? The only remembrance her riches have left are a few hiding-places for lizards and scorpions. The proud merchants of Ormuz showered no wealth on the adjoining country; instead of becoming princes in the land, they have dwindled into half-famished pirates. Their capital has not prevented their city from becoming a den of thieves, the abode of wretchedness and want. Florence, when a great commercial city, when her citizens were rioting in all the luxuriance of wealth, saw her uncultivated fields stagnating in marshes, or withering under the load of heath; it was only when her capital had disappeared, when her industry, awaking from its dream of commercial riches, gave itself to wiser pursuits, that her barren soil was converted into a garden of Eden. They were poor monks living on charity, with no capital but their hands, who placed on the brow of the Apennines their noble crown of forest trees. Venice was great when her nobles were poor; as their fortunes grew her power declined. Holland has lost her capital and her commerce; yet the rebuilding of her cities, and the draining of her lakes, shew that her riches are nothing impaired.

The Jews are a money-getting people; they have for centuries been the usurers of the world ; all their thoughts have been turned to the accumulation of capital. Their object has been pursued with talent and perseverance; their penury is proverbial, and their savings have never been allowed to remain idle. There is not a state whose wants they have not relieved; they have been parties to every scheme for increasing the wealth of nations ; they have sat upon and hatched the golden eggs of all the politicians of Europe. But what has been the fruit of all this grasping and all this hoarding ? Where are the treasures they have heaped up, where the property that calls them lord ? This people of capitalists, this nation of boundless gains, is yet the most beggarly race in existence: for cut off from all connexion with the land, and reduced to traffic in imaginary riches, their profits have never acquired the consistency of property. Wasting their labour on ideal acquisitions, they have sowed the wind and reaped the gossamer. The experience of all times may indeed assure us, that the prosperity soon fades and passes away which has not struck root in the soil; it is then only it brings forth a harvest of plenty. There is no true greatness it will tell us for nations, but in the number and character of their people ; no true wealth but in the abundance and general diffusion of comforts.

Statesmen, if ye be wise, if ye seek the well being of those who are committed to your charge, if ye will that your name shall go down glorious to after ages, ye must cast away from you your books of vain science, and peruse the great volume of Nature. From it ye will learn the vanity of accumulation, it will teach you that plenty is given to man, not to hoard, but for enjoyment. If instead of

reading lectures to Nature, and idly striving to improve
her processes, ye will bend your wisdom to work out her
decrees, science may, indeed, sneer at your labours, and
Political Economy may laugh them to scorn, but the gratitude of a happy people shall be poured out in blessings on
your heads, and heavenly pens shall inscribe your names
in the great Book of Life, where are remembered all the
benefactors to mankind.

THE END.